Lab Manual for MCTS Guide to Microsoft® Windows Server® 2008 Active Directory Configuration

Greg Tomsho

COURSE TECHNOLOGY
CENGAGE Learning™

Australia • Brazil • Japan • Korea • Mexico • Singapore • Spain • United Kingdom • United States

COURSE TECHNOLOGY
CENGAGE Learning™

**Lab Manual for MCTS Guide to Microsoft®
Windows Server® 2008 Active Directory
Configuration**
Author: Greg Tomsho

Vice President, Career and Professional Editorial:
Dave Garza

Executive Editor: Stephen Helba

Acquisitions Editor: Nick Lombardi

Managing Editor: Marah Bellegarde

Senior Product Manager: Michelle Ruelos
Cannistraci

Editorial Assistant: Sarah Pickering

Vice President, Career and Professional Marketing:
Jennifer Ann Baker

Marketing Director: Deborah S. Yarnell

Senior Marketing Manager: Erin Coffin

Associate Marketing Manager: Shanna Gibbs

Production Director: Carolyn Miller

Production Manager: Andrew Crouth

Content Project Manager: Allyson Bozeth

Art Director: Jack Pendleton

Cover designer: Getty Images

Cover photo or illustration: Getty Images

Text designer:

Production Technology Analyst: Jamison MacLachlan

Manufacturing Coordinator: Denise Powers

Copyeditor: Kathy Orrino

Proofreader: Sarah Truax

Compositor: KnowledgeWorks Global Ltd.

© 2011 Course Technology, Cengage Learning

For product information and technology assistance, contact us at
Cengage Learning Customer & Sales Support, 1-800-354-9706

For permission to use material from this text or product,
submit all requests online at **www.cengage.com/permissions**
Further permissions questions can be emailed to
permissionrequest@cengage.com

Example: Microsoft ® is a registered trademark of the Microsoft Corporation.

Library of Congress Control Number: 2010921126

ISBN-13: 978-1-111-12848-7
ISBN-10: 1-111-12848-0

Course Technology
20 Channel Center Street
Boston, MA 02210
USA

Cengage Learning is a leading provider of customized learning solutions with office
locations around the globe, including Singapore, the United Kingdom, Australia,
Mexico, Brazil, and Japan. Locate your local office at: **international.cengage.com/
region**

Cengage Learning products are represented in Canada by
Nelson Education, Ltd.

For your lifelong learning solutions, visit **course.cengage.com**
Visit our corporate website at **cengage.com**.

Some of the product names and company names used in this book have been used
for identification purposes only and may be trademarks or registered trademarks of
their respective manufacturers and sellers.

Microsoft and the Office logo are either registered trademarks or trademarks of Microsoft Corporation in the United States and/or other countries. Course Technology,
a part of Cengage Learning, is an independent entity from the Microsoft Corporation,
and not affiliated with Microsoft in any manner.

Any fictional data related to persons or companies or URLs used throughout this
book is intended for instructional purposes only. At the time this book was printed,
any such data was fictional and not belonging to any real persons or companies.

Course Technology and the Course Technology logo are registered trademarks used
under license.

Course Technology, a part of Cengage Learning, reserves the right to revise this publi-
cation and make changes from time to time in its content without notice.

The programs in this book are for instructional purposes only. They have been tested
with care, but are not guaranteed for any particular intent beyond educational purposes. The author and the publisher do not offer any warranties or representations,
nor do they accept any liabilities with respect to the programs.

Printed in the United States of America
1 2 3 4 5 6 7 14 13 12 11 10

Contents

Introduction

The objective of this Lab Manual is to provide you with hands-on activities that will help prepare you for the Microsoft Certified Technology Specialist (MCTS) exam 70-640: Windows Server 2008 Active Directory, Configuring. This manual is intended to be used along with the Course Technology book *MCTS Guide to Microsoft Windows Server 2008 Active Directory Configuration.*

Note: Exam 70-640 is being deprecated and will be replaced by Exam 83-640. The exam objectives have not changed, but the format of the exam has changed. Exam 83-640 contains a performance-based component in addition to standard exam item types. The performance-based items are hands-on tasks that must be completed by the test-taker.

The activities in this book can be completed by students within a classroom or individually with access to the proper equipment. For the optimal amount of hands-on experience, students will complete the activities in the textbook as well as the activities in this Lab Manual. However, these labs were designed to be completed apart from the activities in the textbook, so students can complete the activities in the textbook in one environment and the activities in this manual in a different environment if desired.

Ideally, these labs will be performed in a virtual machine environment so that students do not require multiple sets of computer hardware or lab partners. However, there is no reason the labs cannot be completed using multiple physical computers connected to a LAN. The labs are written from the perspective of a single student completing all of the steps in an activity.

Features

This lab manual includes the following features to provide an optimal learning experience:

- Lab Objectives—The learning objective and goal of each lab is stated at the beginning of each activity.

- Materials Required—Every lab includes information on the hardware and software needed to complete the lab.

- Estimated Completion Time—Every lab contains an estimated completion time, to help students organize their lab time effectively.

- Activity Background—Activity Background information provides important details for each lab and places the lab activity within the context of the learning objectives.

- Activity Sections—Labs are presented in manageable sections and include figures to reinforce learning.

- Step-by-Step instructions—When a particular task is presented for the first time, step-by-step instructions are provided to complete the activity. However, if a task has already been presented in an earlier lab, the instructions are more generalized (e.g., if a user account is to be created, and user accounts have been created in previous labs, the instruction might simply state 'Create a user account named Jane Doe.').

- Certification Exam Objectives—For each chapter, the relevant exam objectives are listed.

- Review Questions—Review questions that reinforce a student's understanding of the completed activity are provided for each lab.

System Requirements

Several labs require two operating systems to be running simultaneously and Lab 11.2 requires three operating systems to be running simultaneously. These can be running on separate physical computers or they can be running as virtual machines in a host operating system. The use of virtualization is highly recommended. See the Appendix in the textbook, *MCTS Guide to Microsoft Windows Server 2008 Active Directory Configuration,* (ISBN: 1423902351), for more information on using virtualization.

Computer Requirements Using Virtualization

The following tables list the hardware requirements for the host workstation and the virtual machines when virtualization is used. Specific requirements for the chosen virtualization software may vary. Please see the Appendix in the textbook, *MCTS Guide to Microsoft Windows Server 2008 Active Directory Configuration* (ISBN: 1423902351), for virtualization software options.

Virtualization Host System Requirements

Operating System	Suitable operating system to run the chosen virtualization software. Windows XP, Windows Vista, Windows 7, Windows Server 2003, Windows Server 2008, Mac OS X, and various Linux distributions all run virtualization software and can be used.
CPU	Pentium 4 1.8 GHz minimum; Dual core CPU of at least 1.6 GHz recommended. CPU requirements will vary depending upon the virtualization software used.
Memory	2 GB RAM minimum for most labs
Drives	Hard drive with at least 50 GB free, DVD-ROM
Networking	Network interface card. A connection to the Internet is recommended but not required.
Display and peripheral	SVGA or better monitor; bigger is better for working with multiple virtual machines; dual monitors are ideal but not necessary; keyboard and mouse

Virtual Machine Requirements

Virtual Machine Name	Requirements
Server1XX	512 MB RAM 40 GB virtual disk to install Windows Server 2008 Second virtual disk of 5 GB or larger Virtual network interface
Server2XX	512 MB RAM 40 GB virtual disk to install Windows Server 2008 Virtual network interface
ServerCoreXX	512 MB RAM 40 GB virtual disk to install Windows Server 2008 Virtual network interface
ClientXX	1 GB RAM 40 GB virtual disk to install Windows Vista Virtual network interface

Computer Requirements Using Physical Computers

A minimum of two physical computers is required for most labs when not using virtualization. Lab 11.2 requires three machines to be running simultaneously. Server2XX and ServerCoreXX can be installed on a single physical machine in a dual-boot configuration. Each machine has the following minimum requirements:

Computer Name	Requirements
Server1XX	512 MB RAM 40 GB disk to install Windows Server 2008 Second unallocated disk Network interface Super VGA, keyboard, mouse
Server2XX	512 MB RAM 40 GB disk to install Windows Server 2008 Second unallocated disk of at least 40 GB to install ServerCoreXX if using dual boot Network interface Super VGA, keyboard, mouse
ServerCoreXX	512 MB RAM 40 GB disk to install Windows Server 2008 Server Core Network interface Super VGA, keyboard, mouse
ClientXX	1 GB RAM 40 GB virtual disk to install Windows Vista Network interface Super VGA, keyboard, mouse

Software Requirements

- Windows Server 2008, Enterprise Edition
- Windows XP, Vista, or Windows 7 (Labs that include a client workstation use Windows Vista Business, but Windows XP Professional or Windows 7 Professional or Enterprise can be substituted in most cases. The client operating system must support the ability to join a domain)

Note: Windows Server 2008, Windows Vista, and Windows 7 require activation. However, you can leave the product key blank and be granted a 60-day evaluation. You can extend the evaluation for another 60 days up to three times by using the slmgr.vbs program with the −rearm option. From a command prompt, type **slmgr.vbs −xpr** and press **Enter** to view how many days are left on your evaluation. Type **slmgr.vbs −rearm** and press **Enter** to extend the evaluation period for another 60 days.

Lab Setup

Three different Windows Server 2008 installations (two full installations and one Server Core installation) and one Windows Vista installation (or Windows XP or Windows 7) are required to complete all labs. See the following table for the recommended naming convention and IP addressing, and how each server is used:

Installation	Name	IP Address	Usage
Windows Server 2008 Full Installation	Server1XX	192.168.100.1XX 255.255.255.0	Primary server that is used in most labs. Domain controller for domain W2k8ad1XX. local
Windows Server 2008 Full Installation	Server2XX	192.168.100.2XX 255.255.255.0	Used in Chapters 9-13 as a second server to provide a more complex environment for Active Directory, DNS, and other services.
Windows Server 2008 Server Core	ServerCoreXX	192.168.100.XX + 50 255.255.255.0 DNS=192.168.100.1XX when joining to the domain	Used in Chapters 2, 5, 6 and 13 to perform administrative tasks on a Server Core machine.
Vista or similar client	ClientXX (the name is unimportant but must be unique in a classroom network)	192.168.100. XX 255.255.255.0 DNS=192.168.100.1XX when joining to the domain *(The client IP address can also be given via DHCP. It is important that the address not conflict with another computer.)*	As a client computer for testing group policy and other Active Directory procedures.

Note: XX is an assigned student number, so each computer has a unique name in a classroom network. Student numbering should begin with 01; 00 is reserved for the instructor station. The number of students using this scheme cannot exceed 50. If the given IP addressing scheme does not work in your network environment, you can come up with your own, but make sure that no two computers running at the same time share the same address.

The first chapter instructs students to install Windows Server 2008 on two of their lab computers or virtual machines. In Chapter 2, students will be instructed to install Windows Server 2008 Server Core. The installation of the client operating system (Vista, XP, or Windows 7) is not covered in the lab activities but should be available starting in Chapter 5.

Tip: You can download a preconfigured 30-day evaluation of a Windows 7 virtual machine from the Microsoft Web site that works in Microsoft's Virtual PC. Go to www.microsoft.com/downloads and search for "Windows 7 eval."

CHAPTER ONE

INTRODUCING WINDOWS SERVER 2008

Labs included in this chapter

- Lab 1.1 Installing Windows Server 2008 Enterprise Edition (Full Installation) for Server1XX and Server2XX

- Lab 1.2 Completing Initial Tasks for Server1XX and Server2XX

- Lab 1.3 Testing TCP/IP Configuration

- Lab 1.4 Using the License Manager

- Lab 1.5 Working with Server Manager

Microsoft MCTS Exam #70-640 Objectives

Objective

The Chapter 1 labs serve primarily as an introduction to Windows Server 2008 and the initial setup of servers. Thus, the labs do not map directly to exam objectives.

Lab 1.1 Installing Windows Server 2008 Enterprise Edition (Full Installation) for Server1XX and Server2XX

Objectives

- Install Windows Server 2008 Enterprise Edition (Full Installation) on two of the servers you will be using throughout this lab manual. The name of the first server will be Server1XX and the second server will be named Server2XX.

Materials Required

This lab requires the following:

- Two computers or virtual machines that meet the requirements specified under Computer Requirements in the front matter of this book

- A DVD or ISO file for Windows Server 2008 Enterprise Edition

Estimated completion time:	45 minutes or longer (depending on the performance of the system)

Activity Background

Before you can learn about Windows Server 2008, Active Directory, and related topics, you need to install and perform basic configuration options on a Windows Server 2008 server. The installation of Windows Server 2008 is not included in the objectives of the 70-640 exam. However, you will need to perform installations not only in practice, but also in preparation of your lab environment.

Some of the steps and screens in the following lab may vary depending on the installation package you are using.

Activity

1. Power on the first server (which you will name Server1XX) and insert the Windows Server 2008 installation DVD.

2. In the first installation window (Figure 1-1), verify the language, time, and keyboard choices for your environment. Make changes if necessary, and then click **Next**.

3. In the next window, click **Install now**.

4. In the next window, if necessary, enter your product key, and then click **Next**. If you are using the trial version, you can leave the product key blank, but when you click Next, you will be asked if you want to enter your product key now. Click **No** if prompted. (The trial period is good for 60 days but may be extended using slmgr.vbs three times for a total trial period of 240 days.)

5. The next window might differ slightly from Figure 1-2, but you should click **Windows Server 2008 Enterprise (Full Installation)** in the list box, and then click **Next**. If you did not enter a product key on the previous screen, click the check box next to **I have selected the edition of Windows that I purchased** before you click **Next**.

6. If necessary, click the option to accept the license agreement, and then click **Next**. In the Which type of installation do you want? window, click **Custom (advanced)**.

7. In the Where do you want to install Windows? window, click **Drive options (advanced)**. You see a window where you can select options for drive partitions and load drivers for a disk controller. If you simply click Next with an unallocated disk selected, Windows uses the entire disk and formats it as NTFS. Click **Disk 0 Unallocated Space**, and then click **Next**. Now you can just sit back and let Windows

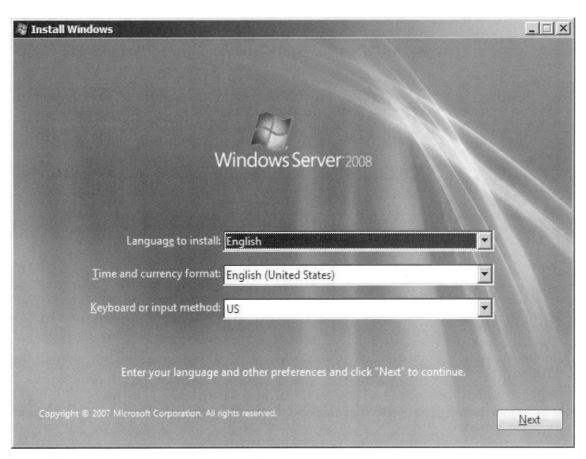

Figure 1-1   The initial installation screen for Windows Server 2008

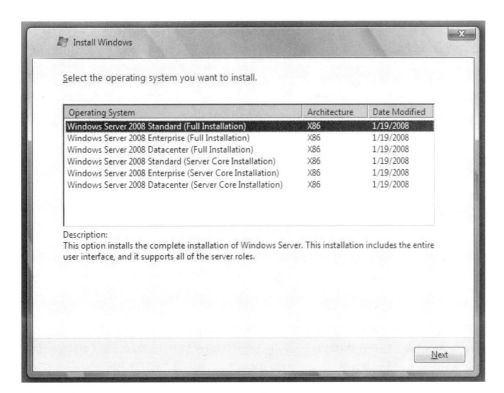

Figure 1-2   Choosing a Full or Server Core installation

The user's password must be changed before logging on the first time.

OK   Cancel

Windows Server 2008
Enterprise

Figure 1-3   After installation, you are prompted to change the Administrator password

do the rest. Your computer restarts at least twice, and then you see the window shown in Figure 1-3. Click **OK**.

8. In the next window, enter **Password01** twice, and then click the arrow to log on. In the message box stating that your password has been changed, click **OK**. After you're logged on, the Initial Configuration Tasks applet is displayed.

9. Power on the second server (which you will name Server2XX) and insert the Windows Server 2008 installation DVD. Follow Steps 2 through 8 above. However, if you are using two physical computers, you must change Step 7 as follows to allow free hard disk space for installation of Server Core and the client operating system on this computer:

> In the Where do you want to install Windows? window, click Drive options (advanced). You see a window where you can select options for drive partitions and load drivers for a disk controller. If you simply click Next with an unallocated disk selected, Windows uses the entire disk and formats it as NTFS. Click **New** to specify a new disk partition. In the Size box, delete the value there and type **25000** to specify 25GB. Click **Apply**. Click to **select Disk 0 Partition 1** (which should show a Total Size of just under 25 GB). Click **Next**. Now you can just sit back and let Windows do the rest. Your computer restarts at least twice, and then you see the window shown in Figure 1-3. Click **OK**.

10. Remain logged on to both servers if you are going on to the next lab. Otherwise, log off.

Review Questions

1. What is the minimum available disk space required to install Windows Server 2008?

   a. 5 GB

   b. 10 GB

   c. 20 GB

   d. 40 GB

2. What happens if you do not enter a product key during installation?

   a. The installation of Windows Server 2008 is cancelled

   b. You are warned that your copy of Windows Server 2008 may be counterfeit

   c. You may use Windows Server 2008 for a 60-day trial period by default

   d. You cannot continue the installation until you enter a product key

3. When do you choose the Administrator password?

   a. Before you choose where to install Windows Server 2008

   b. On the screen after you choose where to install Windows Server 2008

   c. After the installation is complete, but before you log on the first time

   d. After you log on, in the Initial Configuration Tasks applet

4. Why would you want to choose Drive options (advanced) in the Where do you want to install Windows? window? (Choose all that apply.)

   a. To create a partition on which to install Windows Server 2008

   b. To create a RAID volume on which to install Windows Server 2008

   c. To load disk controller drivers

   d. To upgrade an existing operating system

5. On the "Which type of installation do you want? screen," what option is displayed besides Custom (advanced)?

   a. Clean install

   b. Repair

   c. Server Core installation

   d. Upgrade

Lab 1.2 Completing Initial Tasks for Server1XX and Server2XX

Objectives

- Set the server time and time zone for Server1XX and Server2XX
- Configure IP settings, server names, and workgroup names for Server1XX and Server2XX

Materials Required

This lab requires the following:

- The computer or virtual machine that will be named Server1XX
- The computer or virtual machine that will be named Server2XX

Estimated completion time: **20 minutes**

Activity Background

Once Windows Server 2008 is installed, several tasks must be completed before the server is ready to use. Among these tasks are setting the time and time zone, configuring IP address settings, naming the server, and choosing a workgroup or domain of which the server will be a member.

Activity

1. If necessary, log on to Server1XX as Administrator. Your logging on starts the Initial Configuration Tasks applet. (If it doesn't open, click **Start**, **Run**, type **oobe** [which stands for "out-of-box experience"] in the Open text box, and then click **OK**.)

2. Under Provide Computer Information, click **Set time zone** to open the Date and Time dialog box.

3. Click the **Change time zone** button, and select your time zone in the drop-down list. If your region observes daylight saving time, make sure the Automatically adjust clock for Daylight Saving Time check box is selected, and then click **OK**. If the time and date are incorrect, click the **Change date and time** button to modify them, and then click **OK**.

4. Click the **Additional Clocks** tab, where you can tell Windows to display the time in other time zones when you hover your mouse pointer over the taskbar clock.

5. Click the **Internet Time** tab, where you can select the option to synchronize with a time server on the Internet. By default, Windows Server 2008 is set to synchronize with http://time.windows.com, and synchronization occurs weekly. To use a different time server or disable Internet time synchronization, click the **Change settings** button. You can choose from a list of time servers or enter the name of another server. You can also tell Windows to synchronize now by clicking the **Update now** button. If time synchronization isn't working, a firewall might be blocking it.

6. Click **OK** twice to close the Date and Time dialog box.

7. The remainder of tasks will be completed without using the Initial Configuration Tasks applet. Close the Initial Configuration Tasks applet by clicking **Close**. (If you need to open the Initial Configuration Tasks applet again, see Step 1.)

8. By default, when the Initial Configuration Tasks applet is closed, Server Manager starts. To configure the IP address of the server, click **View Network Connections** in the Computer Information section under Server Summary in Server Manager.

9. Right-click **Local Area Connection** and click **Properties** to open the Local Area Connection Properties dialog box (see Figure 1-4).

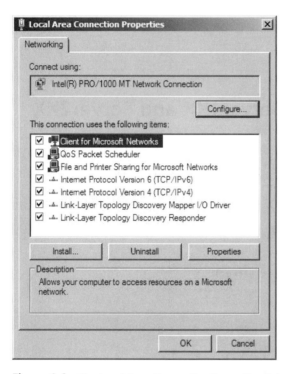

Figure 1-4   The Local Area Connection Properties dialog box

10. Click **Internet Protocol Version 4 (TCP/IPv4)** and click the **Properties** button.

11. In the Internet Protocol Version 4 (TCP/IPv4) Properties dialog box, click the **Use the following IP address** option button (see Figure 1-5). Then, fill in the following information (if you're using an IP addressing scheme that is different from that specified in the lab setup instructions, see your instructor for the IP address values):

   • IP address: **192.168.100.1XX** (replacing XX with your assigned two-digit student number, which your instructor will give you)

   • Subnet mask: **255.255.255.0**

   • Default gateway: **192.168.100.250** (or whatever your network requires)

   • Preferred DNS server: **192.168.100.200** (the address of the classroom server)

   • Alternate DNS server: Leave blank or enter a value specified by your instructor

12. Click **OK**, and then click **Close**.

13. To verify your settings, right-click **Local Area Connection** and click **Status**. Then click the **Details** button to open the Network Connection Details dialog box.

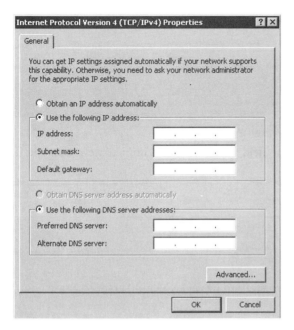

Figure 1-5 Configure IP address settings

14. Verify all the information, and then click **Close**. Click **Close** again.

15. Close the **Network Connections** window.

16. Now, you will change the server name. In Server Manager, Click **Change System Properties**. In the System Properties dialog box, click the **Computer Name** tab, if necessary. Click the **Change** button.

17. In the Computer name text box, type **Server1XX** (replacing XX with your two-digit student number).

18. In the Workgroup text box, type **ADCONFIGCLASS** or another name assigned by your instructor, and then click **OK**. After a moment or two, you should see the message "Welcome to the ADCONFIGCLASS workgroup." Click **OK**. When prompted to restart your computer, click **OK**. Click **Close**, and then click **Restart Now**.

19. When your server restarts, log on. The Initial Configuration Tasks applet should start. If it does not, see Step 1 to start it. Review the information displayed for the time zone, IP address, computer name, and workgroup. If everything looks correct, you are finished with the initial configuration of Server1XX. Close Initial Configuration Tasks.

20. Log on to Server2XX as **Administrator**, if necessary. The Initial Configuration Tasks applet starts. Complete Steps 2 through 19 with the following changes:

    Step 11: Change the IP address to **192.168.100.2XX**.

    Step 17: Change the computer name to **Server2XX**.

21. Stay logged on to both servers if you are going on to the next lab. Otherwise, log off.

Review Questions

1. What can you type in the Start, Run box to run the Initial Configuration Tasks applet?

    a. Inconfig

    b. oobe

    c. mmc

    d. cmd

2. Which of the following tasks is not available in the Initial Configuration Tasks applet?

    a. Setting the time zone

    b. Configuring networking

    c. Activating Windows Server 2008

    d. Changing the computer name

3. Which of the following requires you to restart Windows Server 2008?

   a. Changing the IP address

   b. Activating Windows Server 2008

   c. Setting the time zone

   d. Changing the computer name

4. True or False? TCP/IPv6 is disabled by default on Windows Server 2008.

5. When assigning an IP address to your computer, the field you must fill in immediately after the IP address is the _____ _____.

Lab 1.3 Testing TCP/IP Configuration

Objectives

- Test your network configuration to verify it is correct after Server1XX and Server2XX are configured

Materials Required

This lab requires the following:

- Server1XX and Server2XX
- Classroom server with DNS installed and firewall configured to allow ICMP echo requests

Estimated completion time: **10 minutes**

Activity Background

You have completed installation of Windows Server 2008 and have performed initial configuration tasks. Both of your servers should be connected to a network, whether physical or virtual. To ensure that your configuration is correct, you should test communication between your servers and between your servers and other devices. In this lab, you will start both servers and attempt to ping your DNS server and then each server from the other. Because the Windows Server 2008 firewall blocks ICMP echo requests (incoming Ping packets), you will need to configure the firewall to allow Ping packets.

Activity

1. Start Server1XX and Server2XX and log on to each as Administrator, if necessary.

2. On Server1XX, open a command prompt by clicking **Start** and **Command Prompt**. In the command prompt, type **ipconfig /all** and press **Enter** to view your TCP/IP configuration. Verify that the settings are correct as specified in Lab 1.2.

3. To ping your DNS server, type **ping 192.168.100.200** and press **Enter**. A successful ping will provide results similar to Figure 1-6. If the ping is not successful, review your IP address settings as specified in Lab 1-2.

4. Repeat Steps 2 and 3 for Server2XX. Your results should be similar to Figure 1-6.

5. From the command prompt on Server2XX, type **ping 192.168.100.1XX** (the address of Server1XX) and press **Enter**. This ping attempt should fail because by default Windows Server 2008 blocks incoming Ping packets (ICMP echo requests).

6. To allow ping packets to be received on Server2XX, type **netsh firewall set icmpsetting 8** and press **Enter**. Repeat the same command on Server1XX.

7. From the command prompt on Server2XX, type **ping 192.168.100.1XX** (the IP address of Server1XX) and press **Enter**. You should get four successful replies. From Server1XX, make sure that you can ping the address of Server2XX.

8. Type **ping /?** and press **Enter** to view the options available for the Ping program. Review the available options.

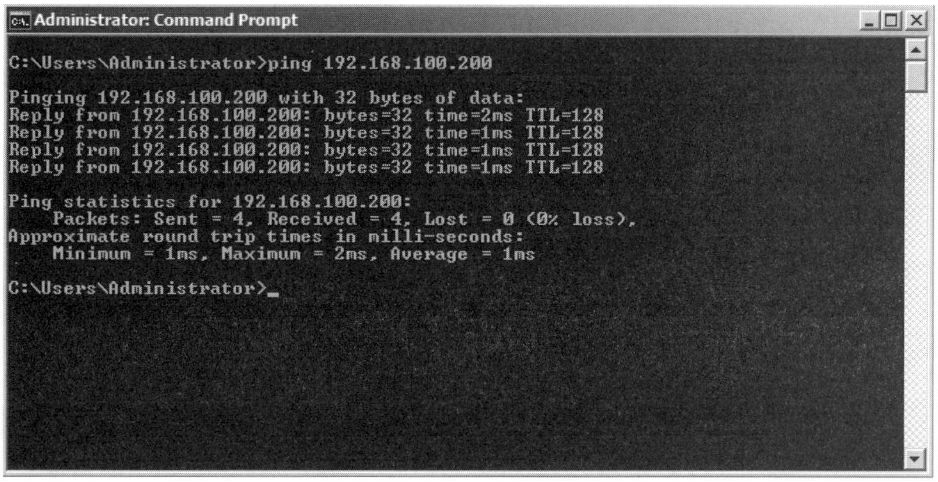

Figure 1-6   Ping results

9. You can instruct ping to attempt to resolve the name of the computer you are trying to ping. On Server1XX, **type ping –a 192.168.100.2XX** and press **Enter**. If ping did not display Server2XX in the first line of output, then it was unable to resolve the name.

10 Shut down Server2XX. Remain logged on to Server1XX if you are going on to the next lab. Otherwise, shut down Server1XX as well.

Review Questions

1. The output of ipconfig /all shows a value called Physical Address, which is a 12-character hexadecimal number. What is another common name for this value?

   a. IP address

   b. MAC address

   c. TCP address

   d. Network address

2. The type of packet that the Ping command sends to another computer is referred to as which of the following?

   a. ICMP echo request

   b. IP echo

   c. ICMP reply

   d. TCP retry

3. Pings to a Windows Server 2008 computer will fail by default for which of the following reasons?

   a. Networking is not configured

   b. All Windows Server 2008 interfaces are disabled

   c. The Windows Server 2008 firewall blocks ICMP echo requests

   d. Windows Server 2008 must be activated before it accepts ping packets

4. What option do you use with the Ping command so that you can specify the number of packets to send?

   a. –a

   b. –t

   c. –#

   d. –n

5. The command you use to allow ICMP echo requests to be received by Windows Server 2008 is _____

Lab 1.4 Using the License Manager

Objectives

- View the options of Windows Software Licensing Management Tool (slmgr.vbs)

Materials Required

This lab requires the following:

- Server1XX

Estimated completion time: **10 minutes**

Activity Background

You have completed installation of Windows Server 2008 and have performed initial configuration tasks and tested network configuration. You need to verify the status of your Windows Server 2008 license. This slmgr. vbs program is a Visual Basic script that allows you to view the status of your license, activate Windows, and extend the period of a trial license among other functions. While you can activate a full installation of Windows Server 2008 using the System Properties control panel, slmgr.vbs is the only method available to you to activate a Server Core installation.

Activity

1. Start Server1XX and log on as Administrator, if necessary.

2. Open a command prompt.

3. At the command prompt, type **slmgr.vbs** and press **Enter**. After a few seconds, a window will open showing the help screen for Windows Software Licensing Management Tool (slmgr.vbs). Read the usage information for the program and the available options. The options are shown with a preceding dash ('-'), however, you can also use a forward slash ('/') before each option. Click **OK** when finished.

4. From the command prompt, type **slmgr.vbs -dlv** and press **Enter**. That command will display the current status of your license. If your license is a trial, the time remaining on the trial will be displayed in the last line of the output, as shown in Figure 1-7. Click **OK**.

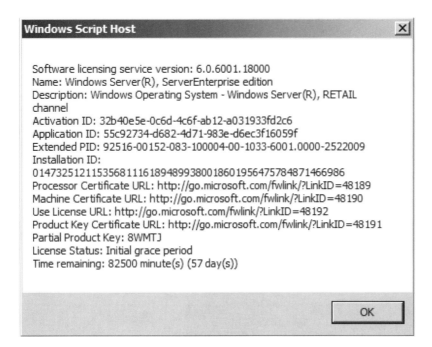

Figure 1-7   Output of the slmgr.vbs -dlv command

5. To view the expiration of your license, type **slmgr.vbs -xpr** and press **Enter**. If your license is a trial, a message indicating the end of the initial grace period is displayed. If your copy of Windows is already activated, a message indicating that is displayed. Click **OK**.

6. If your installation is not a trial and you have already entered the product key but have not yet activated Windows, you can activate Windows by typing **slmgr.vbs -ato**. If you try to activate Windows without having first entered a product key, an error message will be displayed. Type **slmgr.vbs -ato** and press **Enter**. Click **OK** on the message that is displayed. (You may see Windows Script Host flashing in the taskbar if Windows failed to activate; if so, click **Windows Script Host** in the taskbar to display the message box.)

7. If your license is a trial, you can extend the trial period by an additional 60 days up to three times by typing **slmgr.vbs -rearm**. Do not do this now unless your trial is almost expired. Close the command prompt.

8. Remain logged on if you are going on to the next lab. Otherwise, log off.

Review Questions

1. What type of file is slmgr.vbs?

   a. An executable program file

   b. A Visual Basic Script

   c. A Virtual Batch Script

   d. A help file

2. Which of the following are reasons why you would run slmgr.vbs? (Choose all that apply.)

   a. To determine the status of the Windows Server 2008 license

   b. To activate Windows

   c. To send Microsoft registration information

   d. To uninstall a product key

3. True or False? Slmgr.vbs can be used to activate Windows on a Server Core installation.

4. The command to extend the trial period for Windows Server 2008 is _____.

5. You can use slmgr.vbs to extend the initial 60-day trial period in Windows Server 2008 to _____ days.

   a. 120

   b. 180

   c. 240

   d. 360

Lab 1.5 Working with Server Manager

Objectives

- View the features and functions of Server Manager

Materials Required

This lab requires the following:

- Server1XX

Estimated completion time: **10 minutes**

Activity Background

You have completed installation of Windows Server 2008 and have performed initial configuration tasks and tested network configuration. You will soon be putting this server into production but before you do so, you want to become somewhat more familiar with the primary administrative interface, Server Manager. In addition, you may want to manage this server remotely, so you will enable Remote Desktop.

Activity

1. Start Server1XX and log on as Administrator, if necessary. If the Initial Configuration Tasks applet starts, check the **Do not show this window at logon** check box and click the **Close** button. Server Manager should start. If it doesn't, click the **Server** icon on the Quick Launch toolbar.

2. Click **Server Manager (Server1XX)** in the left pane, if necessary. In the right pane are several information sections: Server Summary, Roles Summary, Features Summary, and Resources and Support. There may be one or more sub-sections within each of the main sections. For example, under Server Summary, there is a box for Computer Information and a box for Security Information. Note that you can configure each of the items displayed by clicking the corresponding links located in the upper-right corner of each section.

3. In the Computer Information section, note that Remote Desktop is disabled. To easily configure Remote Desktop, click the **Configure Remote Desktop** link in the upper-right corner of the Computer Information section. The System Properties dialog box opens to the Remote tab. Click the **Allow connections only from computers running Remote Desktop with Network Level Authentication** option button. Click **OK** in the message box explaining that a Remote Desktop Firewall exception will be enabled. Enabling Remote Desktop allows members of the Administrators group access to this server remotely unless you add additional users by clicking Select Users. For now, click **OK**.

4. Review the options listed under Security Information. Notice the last item listed is IE Enhanced Security Configuration (ESC). While IE ESC normally should be enabled on a server, you will turn it off to make Internet access more convenient for these labs. To do so, click **Configure IE ESC** in the box on the right.

5. In the Internet Explorer Enhanced Security Configuration dialog box, click the **Off** option button under Administrators. Leave IE ESC set to On for Users. Click **OK**. This will allow you to browse Web sites more conveniently if necessary.

6. View the information in the Roles Summary and Features Summary boxes. Both of these should indicate that 0 items are installed. In the Resources and Support box, click **Windows Server TechCenter**. If you had left IE ESC turned on for administrators, you would have had to respond to several prompts indicating that the Web site has been blocked. Because you disabled IE ESC, the Microsoft TechNet page should load. You can read more about Server Manager in this TechNet article. Once finished, close Internet Explorer.

7. In the left pane of Server Manager, click the **Roles** node. The right pane shows a summary of the installed roles followed by sections about each installed role. If you don't have any roles installed, you might see only limited information. You begin working with roles in Chapter 3.

8. Click the **Diagnostics** node in the left pane to display three tools for monitoring and solving problems on a server: Event Viewer, Reliability and Performance, and Device Manager. You will learn more about Event Viewer in Chapter 13.

9. Click the **Configuration** node to see five tools for performing configuration and maintenance tasks.

10. Click the **Storage** node. Here you find the Windows Server Backup program and the Disk Management tool that are part of the Computer Management MMC.

11. Close Server Manager and shut down Server1XX.

Review Questions

1. Which of the following is not one of the tools available in the Diagnostics node of Server Manager?

    a. Disk Management

    b. Event Viewer

    c. Reliability and Performance

    d. Device Manager

2. Which of the following is an option for configuring IE ESC? (Choose all that apply.)

   a. Off for Administrators

   b. On for Guests

   c. Off for Users

   d. On for Everyone

3. True or False? Server Manager always starts when you log on to the server, and this feature cannot be disabled.

4. The Windows Firewall with Advanced Security can be found under the _____ node of Server Manager.

5. By default, when you enable remote desktop, which of the following user(s) can access the server using remote desktop?

   a. All members of the Users group

   b. Only the Administrator user

   c. Only the user that enabled Remote Desktop

   d. All members of the Administrators group

CHAPTER TWO

INSTALLING WINDOWS SERVER 2008

Labs included in this chapter

- Lab 2.1 Installing Windows Server 2008 Server Core
- Lab 2.2 Completing Initial Tasks for Server Core
- Lab 2.3 Adding Users and Groups to Server Core and Performing Basic Monitoring Tasks
- Lab 2.4 Performing Basic Remote Management of Server Core

Microsoft MCTS Exam #70-640 Objectives

Objective	Lab
Creating and maintaining Active Directory objects	2.3

Lab 2.1 Installing Windows Server 2008 Server Core

Objectives

- Install Windows Server 2008 Enterprise Edition Server Core

Materials Required

This lab requires the following:

- A computer or virtual machine that meets the requirements specified under Computer Requirements in the front matter of this book. If you will be using physical computers for this installation and you have only two computers, it is recommended that you use unallocated disk space on Server2XX for this installation.
- A DVD or ISO file for Windows Server 2008 Enterprise Edition

Estimated completion time: **30 minutes or longer (depending on the performance of the system)**

Activity Background

Windows Server 2008 offers two installation options for each edition: Full Installation and Server Core. Server Core has a minimal graphical user interface (GUI) and is primarily managed from the command line on the local server or remotely. Server Core is an excellent installation option when a server will be located at a branch office or when it will be running as a virtual machine due to its lower resource requirements.

Activity

1. Power on the server and insert the Windows Server 2008 installation DVD.
2. In the first installation window, verify the language, time, and keyboard choices for your environment. Make changes if necessary, and then click **Next**.
3. Click **Install now**. If necessary, enter your product key, and then click **Next**. (If you are using a trial version of Windows Server 2008, leave the product key blank, and click **No** to the ensuing prompt.)
4. Click **Windows Server 2008 Enterprise (Server Core Installation)** in the list box, and then click **Next**.
5. If necessary, click the option to accept the license agreement, and then click **Next**. In the Which type of installation do you want? window, click **Custom (advanced)**, and then click **Next**.
6. In the Where do you want to install Windows? window, click **Disk 0 Unallocated Space**, and then click **Next**.
7. When the installation is finished, press **Ctrl+Alt+Delete** as prompted to log on.
8. Click the **Other User** icon. In the User name text box, type **Administrator**, and then click the arrow next to Password prompt. (Don't enter a password at this time; the initial password for Administrator is blank.)
9. In the next window, you're prompted to change the user's password. Click **OK**.
10. Type **Password01** in the New password text box and the Confirm password text box.
11. Click the arrow next to the Confirm password text box. When you see a message that the password has been changed, click **OK**. You're now logged on.
12. One item you may want to set immediately on Server Core is the screensaver timeout. By default it is 10 minutes. The only way to do this from the Server Core computer is to edit the registry. Thankfully, the graphical regedt32 program is among the few graphical programs that run on Server Core. From the command line, type **regedt32** and press **Enter** to start Registry Editor.
13. Click to expand the HKEY_CURRENT_USER folder and continue to expand folder until you get to the path HKEY_CURRENT_USER\Control Panel\Desktop. Click **Desktop** in the left pane of Registry Editor and find the ScreenSaveTimeOut value in the right pane (see Figure 2-1). Double-click **ScreenSaveTimeOut**. In the Value data box, type **3600** and click **OK**. The value specifies the number of seconds before the

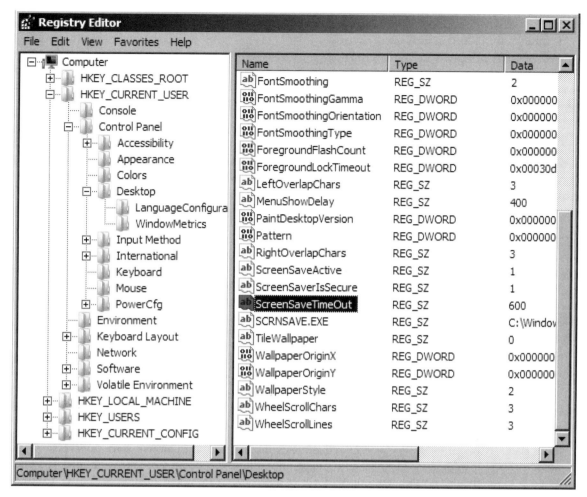

Figure 2-1   Registry Editor – ScreenSaveTimeOut key

screensaver is activated. A value of 3600 indicates an hour. Alternately, you can disable the screensaver by changing the value of ScreenSaveActive from 1 to 0.

14. Close the Registry Editor and stay logged on for the next lab.

Review Questions

1. True or False? A Server Core installation requires more disk and memory resources than a full installation.

2. When you first log on to Server Core, which of the following is available?

   a. Start menu

   b. Command prompt

   c. Task bar

   d. All of the above

3. Server Core might be a good installation option for a(n) _____. (Choose all that apply.)

   a. branch office server

   b. first server in your network

   c. application server

   d. virtual machine

4. Which of the following runs in a Server Core installation?

   a. Registry editor

   b. Microsoft Management Console

    c. Server Manager

    d. Initial Configuration Tasks

5. When logged on to Server Core, most configuration tasks require you to use the _____ _____.

Lab 2.2 Completing Initial Tasks for Server Core

Objective

- Complete the initial configuration tasks for a Server Core installation

Materials Required

This lab requires the following:

- The server or virtual machine that will become ServerCoreXX

Estimated completion time:	**20 minutes**

Activity Background

You have just completed installing Server Core. You will now complete the same initial configuration tasks as you completed for your full installation servers. Server Core requires these tasks to be completed using command-line programs.

Activity

1. Log on to Server Core as Administrator, if necessary.

2. Since the only user interface to Server Core is the command prompt, you will learn how to start a new command prompt if you close it. If the command prompt window is open, close it by typing **exit** and pressing **Enter** or by clicking the **X** at the upper-right corner of the command prompt window. You now have a blank desktop.

3. Press **Ctrl+Alt+Delete** to open the window shown in Figure 2-2. Click the arrow next to Start Task Manager.

Figure 2-2   The Ctrl+Alt+Delete menu

4. In Windows Task Manager, click **File**, **New Task (Run)** from the menu.

5. In the Create New Task dialog box, type **cmd** and click **OK**. The command prompt window is restored.

6. Close Windows Task Manager, but leave the command prompt window open for the next steps.

7. To set the time, type **timedate.cpl** and press **Enter**. This command opens the Date and Time dialog box, one of two available in Server Core. (The other one is Regional and Language Options, which you can access by typing **intl.cpl** and pressing **Enter**.)

8. Change the date, time, and time zone as needed, and then click **OK**.

9. To set a static IP address, type **ipconfig /all | more** and press **Enter**. Make a note of the default gateway and preferred DNS server that have been assigned. If necessary, press the **spacebar** to see the rest of the output from the ipconfig command (you may have to press the spacebar more than once).

10. Before you can run commands to set IP address information, you need some information about your network interfaces. At the command prompt, type **netsh interface ipv4 show interfaces** and press **Enter**. You should get an output similar to Figure 2-3.

Figure 2-3 Output from the netsh interface command

11. Note the number in the Idx column of the Local Area Connection row. In Figure 2-3 this number is 2. You need this number for the next commands.

12. Next, type **netsh interface ipv4 set address name="n" source=static address=192.168.100.XX+50 mask=255.255.255.0 gateway=192.168.100.250** and press **Enter**. (Replace the n in name="n" with the value you noted from Step 11; replace XX+50 with your 2-digit student number plus 50 and the gateway address with whatever is appropriate for your network.)

13. To set the DNS server address, type **netsh interface ipv4 add dnsserver name="n" address=192.168.100.200 index=1** and press **Enter** (replacing the *n* after "name" with the value you noted from Step 11; the address should be replaced with the value appropriate for your network). If you had a secondary DNS server to add, you would use the same command but use the secondary DNS server's IP address and change the number after "index" to 2.

14. Verify the information by typing **ipconfig /all** and pressing **Enter**. Check that all addresses are correct for the IP addressing scheme you are using.

15. To set the computer name and workgroup name of the server, type **hostname** and press **Enter**. Make a note of the hostname, which probably starts with WIN. You need to specify the entire hostname in the next step.

16. Type **netdom renamecomputer** *computername* **/newname:ServerCore***XX* and press **Enter** (replacing *computername* with the hostname you noted in Step 15 and *XX* with your two-digit student number). When asked whether you want to proceed, type **y** and press **Enter**.

17. To complete the name change, you must restart the computer. Type **shutdown /r /t 0** and press **Enter**. The /r option specifies a computer restart, and the /t 0 option specifies restarting in 0 seconds (that is, immediately).

18. After your computer has restarted, log on to your server as **Administrator**.

19. Oddly enough, changing the workgroup name involves using a different command environment. This command environment is called Windows Management Instrumentation Command-line; each command is preceded with "wmic." Type **wmic computersystem where name="ServerCore***XX***" call joindomainorworkgroup name="ADCONFIGCLASS"** (replacing *XX* with your student number) and press **Enter**.

20. The workgroup name isn't displayed by using the ipconfig command. To display your NetBIOS name and workgroup name, type **nbtstat -n** and press **Enter**. The workgroup name is shown in the Name column in the row listing GROUP in the Type column.

21. Leave the command prompt window open for the next lab.

Review Questions

1. To start a command prompt in Server Core when none is currently open, you must do the following.

    a. Right-click Computer and click Run Command Prompt

    b. Right-click the desktop, click Run, and type cmd

    c. Power off the server and power it back on

    d. Press Ctrl+Alt+Delete and start Task Manager

2. Which initial configuration task can be completed using a GUI in Server Core?

    a. Setting the time zone

    b. Setting the IP address

    c. Changing the computer name

    d. Configuring Windows Update

3. Which command displays detailed network interface configuration information?

    a. ipconfig /more

    b. ipconfig /all

    c. netsh /showall

    d. netsh /detail

4. True or False? To join your Server Core computer to a workgroup, type netdom join *workgroup*.

5. To set the time using a GUI on Server Core, you should type _____.

Lab 2.3 Adding Users and Groups to Server Core and Performing Basic Monitoring Tasks

Objectives

- Create users and groups on Windows Server 2008 Server Core
- View and manage event logs and services

Materials Required

This lab requires the following:

- ServerCoreXX

Estimated completion time: **10 minutes**

Activity Background

You have installed Windows Server 2008 Server Core and have completed a number of initial post-installation tasks. You want to be able to log on to this server using an account other than Administrator. You also would like to be able to perform basic server monitoring tasks such as viewing and managing the event logs and listing and starting/stopping services. The net command allows you to perform a variety of tasks including management of users and groups on the local computer. The wevtutil program provides command-line management and monitoring of the event log. The sc, tasklist, and taskkill commands are service and process management command-line utilities. Finally, you will explore and use the shutdown command, which allows you to turn off and restart the system with a variety of options.

Activity

1. Log on to ServerCoreXX as Administrator, and open a command prompt if necessary.

2. To list current members of the local Administrators group, type **net localgroup administrators** and press **Enter** at the command prompt. The output of this command includes the description of the group and a list of its members. In this case, the Administrator account is the only member.

3. To create a new user with a logon name of adminuser, type **net user adminuser * /add** and press **Enter**. You are prompted to enter a password. Type **Password01** (or a password of your choice) and press **Enter**. Type the password again when prompted and press **Enter**.

4. To add adminuser to the local Administrators group, type **net localgroup administrators adminuser /add** and press **Enter**. To verify that adminuser is now a member of the Administrators group, type **net localgroup administrators** and press **Enter**. The list of members should now include adminuser.

5. To view a list of event logs, type **wevtutil el** and press **Enter**. The output of this command produces a long list of event logs available to display.

6. To view all events in the System event log, type **wevtutil qe System /f:text** and press **Enter**. A long list of events is displayed. To see one screen of output at a time, type **wevtutil qe System /f:text | more** and press **Enter**. Many options exist for the wevtutil command. To get help on this command type **wevtutil /help** and press **Enter**.

7. To view a list of running services, type **sc query** and press **Enter**. A list of all services is displayed. You can also specify a particular service to query its status by including the service name at the end of the command. For example, to display information about DNS, you can type sc query DNS. To display the currently running processes, type **tasklist** and press **Enter**.

8. If you need to stop a running process, the taskkill command can be used. You must retrieve the process ID (PID) using the tasklist command first. From the output of the tasklist command you just entered, find the cmd.exe process. Find the number in the PID column. Type **taskkill /PID** *pid* and press **Enter** where *pid* is the process ID shown for the cmd.exe process.

9. Your command prompt should have just closed. Review Steps 3-6 of Lab 2.2 to restore your command prompt.

10. At the command prompt, type **shutdown /?**. Review some of the options for the shutdown command. The /s parameter shuts the computer down. The /r parameter restarts the computer. The /t parameter indicates the period of time before the command should take affect. The /d parameter allows you to specify the reason the server is being shut down. Type **shutdown /s /t 0** and press **Enter**.

Review Questions

1. The command to create a new user named joe on the local server is _____.

   a. dsadd user joe *

   b. net user joe * /add

   c. netadd /user joe *

   d. dsadd /user joe *

2. To add a user named joe to a group named Marketing on the local computer, you should use which command?

   a. net localgroup Marketing joe /add

   b. net localgroup joe /add Marketing

   c. net user /add localgroup Marketing joe

   d. net user joe /add localgroup Marketing

3. To display information about a service named dhcp, type _____.

4. True of False? To end a process named dhcp, type taskkill dhcp.

5. To restart your server in ten seconds, you should type _____.

Lab 2.4 Performing Basic Remote Management of Server Core

Objectives

- Configure server core firewall settings to allow you to test network connectivity using ping
- Configure server core firewall to allow remote desktop connections

Materials Required

This lab requires the following:

- The Server1XX and ServerCoreXX servers

Estimated completion time: **15 minutes**

Activity Background

Because the Windows Server 2008 firewall blocks ICMP echo requests (incoming Ping packets), you will need to configure the firewall to allow Ping packets so you can ping ServerCoreXX from another computer. Then you will configure the firewall to allow remote desktop connections.

Activity

1. Start Server1XX and ServerCoreXX and log on to each as Administrator, if necessary.

2. On ServerCoreXX, open a command prompt if necessary.

3. To verify that you can ping Server1XX successfully, type **ping 192.168.100.1XX** (the address of Server1XX) and press **Enter**. If the ping was not successful, verify the IP address settings on both servers to ensure they match the address scheme you are using.

4. On ServerCoreXX, type **netsh firewall set icmpsetting 8** and press **Enter** to allow incoming ping packets to ServerCoreXX.

5. Open a command prompt on Server1XX. Type **ping 192.168.100.XX+50** (ServerCoreXX's IP address) and press **Enter**. The ping should be successful. If it is not, verify the IP address settings on both servers to ensure they match the address scheme you are using.

6. Next, you will configure ServerCoreXX to allow remote desktop connections. At the command prompt on ServerCoreXX, type **cscript C:\windows\system32\scregedit.wsf /ar /v** and press **Enter**. This command displays the current remote desktop settings. The 1 in the output indicates that remote desktop connections are denied.

7. Type **cscript C:\windows\system32\scregedit.wsf /ar 0** and press **Enter**. This command changes the setting to 0, which allows remote desktop connections. Type the command from Step 6 again to verify the setting has been changed to 0.

8. You must also enable remote desktop connections through the firewall. Type **netsh advfirewall firewall set rule group="Remote Desktop" new enable=yes** and press **Enter**.

9. From Server1XX, click **Start** and type **mstsc** in the Start Search box and press **Enter**. This command starts a terminal services client connection (remote desktop). In the text box, type **192.168.100.XX+50** (ServerCoreXX's IP address) and click **Connect**.

10. When prompted to enter your credentials, type **Administrator** in the User name box and **Password01** in the Password box and press **OK**. A remote desktop connection is established and you should see the command prompt for the ServerCoreXX server. You can now manage the ServerCoreXX server as if you were logged on to the local console. Look at the screen on the ServerCoreXX server. Note that the CTRL+ALT+DELETE screen is displayed. You cannot be logged onto server core through both remote desktop and from the console at the same time.

11. To end your remote desktop session with **ServerCoreXX**, type **logoff** and press **Enter**.

12. Log back into **ServerCoreXX** from the console as administrator for the next part of this lab.

13. Another method to manage ServerCoreXX remotely is to use Windows Remote Management (WinRM). WinRM has two parts, WinRM is configured on the computer that will be managed, and Windows Remote Shell (WinRS) is run on the computer from which you will manage the server. Enable WinRM on ServerCoreXX by typing **WinRM quickconfig** and press **Enter**. You see a message stating that WinRM is not set up on this machine and you will be prompted to make the necessary changes to configure WinRM. Press **y** and **Enter**.

14. WinRM is now configured; however, by default WinRM allows only Windows Remote Shell connections when both computers are in the same domain. Because ServerCoreXX and Server1XX are not members of a domain, the connection will fail. To verify this, from a command prompt on Server1XX, type **winrs -r:192.168.100.XX+50 cmd.exe** and press **Enter**. An error message is displayed.

15. In Lab 3.1 when you join ServerCoreXX to the domain you create on Server1XX, you will be able to run this command. Shut down both servers.

Review Questions

1. The command used to start the remote desktop application is _____.
   a. rdp
   b. netsh rdp
   c. mstsc
   d. netsh mstsc

2. Which of the following is the user interface you get when you connect to a Server Core computer using remote desktop?
   a. The user interface of the computer from which you are connecting
   b. A Windows Server 2008 full installation user interface
   c. The standard server core user interface
   d. A server core user interface with the addition of Computer and Recycle Bin desktop icons

3. To end a remote desktop session with server core, type _____.

4. True or False? You run WinRS on a Server Core computer so that you can manage it remotely.

5. Which of the following commands is used to configure Server Core to allow remote desktop connections?
   a. WinRS
   b. WinRM
   c. mstsc
   d. cscript

INTRODUCING ACTIVE DIRECTORY

Labs included in this chapter

- Lab 3.1 Installing Active Directory Domain Services and Joining a Server Core Server

- Lab 3.2 Explore Active Directory and Create New Objects

- Lab 3.3 Using the Command Line and Batch Files to Create Active Directory Objects

- Lab 3.4 Create, Publish, and Find a Shared Folder in Active Directory

- Lab 3.5 Browsing and Using Group Policies

Microsoft MCTS Exam #70-640 Objectives

Objective	Lab
Configuring the Active Directory Infrastructure	3.1, 3.2
Creating and Maintaining Active Directory Objects	3.2, 3.3, 3.4, 3.5

Lab 3.1 Installing Active Directory Domain Services and Joining a Server Core Server

Objectives
- Install Active Directory Domain Services on Server1XX
- Join ServerCoreXX to the domain as a member server

Materials Required
This lab requires the following:
- Server1XX to install Active Directory Domain Services
- ServerCoreXX to be joined to the domain

Estimated completion time: **30 minutes or longer** (depending on the performance of the system)

Activity Background
You are ready to install the first domain controller in a new Active Directory forest. You will install the Active Directory Domain Services role on Server1XX. Because Active Directory requires DNS to function properly, the DNS role will also be installed on Server1XX. Once you have a working domain controller, you can join one of your other servers, ServerCoreXX, to the domain. Once ServerCoreXX is a member of the domain, you can use the WinRS program to remotely access the ServerCoreXX command prompt without using remote desktop.

Activity
1. Start Server1XX and log on as Administrator, if necessary. If the Initial Configuration Tasks applet starts, click the **Do not show this window at logon** check box, and then close the window. Server Manager should start. If it doesn't, click the **Server Manager** icon on the Quick Launch toolbar.

2. In Server Manager, click the **Roles** node in the left pane, and then click **Add Roles**. The next window is informational and warns you to be sure the Administrator account has a strong password, your network settings are configured, and the latest security updates are installed. Click **Next**.

3. In the Select Server Roles window, click **Active Directory Domain Services**, and then click **Next**.

4. Read the information in the next window, which explains that having two domain controllers is optimal, DNS must be installed on the network, and you must run Dcpromo.exe to complete the AD DS installation. Click **Next**.

5. A message is displayed, stating that the server might need to restart and that Dcpromo.exe must be run after the wizard is finished. Click **Install**.

6. You see the Installation Progress window while the role is installed. Once installation completes, the Installation Results window tells you what roles were installed and displays status messages for services that were installed. Click **Close**.

7. Click **Start**, type **dcpromo** in the Start Search text box, and press **Enter**. The Active Directory Domain Services Installation Wizard starts. Click **Next**.

8. You might see a window with compatibility information that explains older OSs could have difficulty authenticating to a Windows Server 2008 domain controller. If so, click **Next**.

9. Click the **Create a new domain in a new forest** option button, and then click **Next**.

10. Next, you will name the forest root domain by entering the new domain's FQDN. Type **W2k8AD1XX. local** (where *XX* is your two-digit student number), and then click **Next**.

11. Next, you will select the forest functional level. To take advantage of new features in Windows Server 2008, you must select the Windows Server 2008 level. Click the list arrow, click **Windows Server 2008**, and then click **Next**.

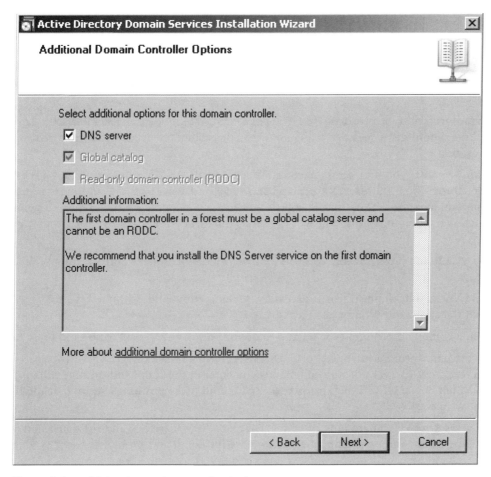

Figure 3-1 Additional Domain Controller Options

12. In the Additional Domain Controller Options window (see Figure 3-1), you will choose whether to install DNS. You can also decide whether this DC should be a global catalog server or an RODC. The option to install a global catalog server is disabled for the first DC in a new forest, and the option to install an RODC is disabled for the first DC in a domain. Ensure that the DNS server check box is checked and click **Next**. (If a message box is displayed explaining that an IP address is dynamically assigned, click **Yes**. This message appears because the IPv6 address on the server is dynamic rather than static. Disabling IPv6 or assigning a static address would prevent this message from appearing.)

13. In the message box explaining that a delegation for this DNS server can't be created, click **Yes**.

14. You can choose locations for the database folder, log files, and SYSVOL folder. Specifying different disks for the database and log files is ideal, but leave the defaults for now. Click **Next**.

15. When asked for a Directory Services Restore Mode password, enter **Password01** in both places. You can use a different password than the Administrator password, if you like. Click **Next**.

16. Review your choices and go back and make changes if necessary. Otherwise, click **Next**.

17. Click **Finish**, and then click **Restart Now** when prompted.

18. After your computer restarts, log on as Administrator. Open **Server Manager**, if necessary, and verify the domain information that's displayed. Some new messages have been created during installation. You can ignore them for now.

19. Click **Start** and point to **Administrative Tools**. Note some of the new MMCs that have been added: Active Directory Domains and Trusts, Active Directory Sites and Services, Active Directory Users and Computers, ADSI Edit, Group Policy Management, and DNS.

20. Close all open windows.

21. Next, you will join ServerCoreXX to the W2k8AD1XX.local domain. Start ServerCoreXX if necessary and log on as Administrator.

22. First, change the DNS server address of ServerCoreXX to the address of Server1XX. Type **netsh interface ipv4 add dnsserver name="n" address=192.168.100.1XX index=1** and press **Enter**. This is the same command you entered in Step 13 of Lab 2.2, except the address is the address of Server1XX. Be sure to replace the 'n' after 'name=' with the number you used in Step 12 of Lab 2.2. Note that this command does not replace the existing DNS server address, but instead makes the new address the primary DNS server.

23. From the command prompt, type **netdom join ServerCoreXX /domain:W2k8AD1XX.local** and press **Enter**. You should get a message explaining that the computer needs to be restarted in order to complete the operation.

24. Type **shutdown /r /t 0** and press **Enter**. When ServerCoreXX reboots, click **Switch User** and click **Other User**. Type **W2k8AD1XX\administrator** and **Password01** and press **Enter** to log on as the domain administrator. Note that if you do not include the domain name when logging onto a member computer as the administrator, you will log on as the local administrator rather than the domain administrator.

25. Type **ipconfig /all** and press **Enter**. You will see that your primary DNS suffix is now W2k8AD1XX.local.

26. Log on to Server1XX as the administrator if necessary. Open a command prompt. Type **cd ** and press **Enter**. Note that the command prompt changes to C:\>.

27. To remotely open a command prompt, type **winrs -r:servercoreXX cmd.exe** and press **Enter**.

28. Note how the command prompt changed to C:\Users\administrator.W2k8AD1XX>. You are now connected to the ServerCoreXX server and any commands you enter in the command prompt will be processed on ServerCoreXX, not Server1XX. Type **ipconfig /all** and press **Enter** to verify that the IP address settings are those of ServerCoreXX.

29. Type **Exit** and press **Enter**. You are now disconnected from ServerCoreXX and the command prompt is on Server1XX. Type **Exit** and press **Enter** again to close the command prompt.

30. If you are going on to the next lab, remain logged on to Server1XX. If you are not going on to the next lab, shut down Server1XX. Shut down ServerCoreXX.

Review Questions

1. True or False? You are finished installing Active Directory Domain Services once the Add Roles wizard finishes.

2. When installing the first domain controller for the first domain in a forest, which option is selected by default and cannot be changed?

   a. Global catalog server

   b. DNS server

   c. RODC

   d. All of the above

3. Which MMCs are added after Active Directory is installed? (Choose all that apply.)

   a. ADSI Edit

   b. Group Policy Management

   c. Active Directory Forests and Trees

   d. Active Directory Sites and Services

4. Before you can add ServerCoreXX as a domain member, you must _____.

   a. change its IP address

   b. change its DNS server address

   c. disable the firewall

   d. run WinRS

5. The command to add ComputerA to Domain1 is _____.

Lab 3.2 Explore Active Directory and Create New Objects

Objectives

- Discover existing Active Directory objects and create OUs, users, and groups

Materials Required

- Server1XX

Estimated completion time: **20 minutes**

Activity Background

With Active Directory installed, you can begin to create Active Directory objects such as OUs, users, and groups. A few important objects that are created during the installation process include the domain object, the Builtin and Users folders, which house the default users and groups, and the Domain Controllers OU, which contains the domain controller computer objects. The Computers folder is also created and is initially empty but is the default location for newly created computer accounts that join the domain.

Activity

1. Start Server1XX and log on as Administrator, if necessary. Server Manager should start. If it doesn't, click the **Server Manager** icon on the Quick Launch toolbar.

2. Open Active Directory Users and Computers by clicking **Start**, pointing to **Administrative Tools**, and clicking **Active Directory Users and Computers**.

3. Click the domain object in the left pane (the object is named W2k8AD1XX.local).

4. If necessary, click **View**, **Detail** from the menu so that objects are displayed in the right pane with their names, types, and descriptions.

5. Right-click the domain object and click **Properties**. Click the **General** tab, if necessary, and note that both the domain functional level and forest functional level are Windows Server 2008.

6. Enter a description for your domain, such as Windows Server 2008 Domain XX, and then click **OK**.

7. Click to expand the domain node, if necessary. Click the **Builtin** folder in the left pane to view its contents a list of group accounts created when Active Directory was installed in the right pane.

8. Click the **Computers** folder in the left pane. A computer account for ServerCoreXX should be in this folder. When a workstation or server joins a domain, its account is automatically created in the Computers folder.

9. Click the **Domain Controllers** OU in the left pane. A computer object representing your domain controller is displayed in the right pane.

10. Right-click the **Domain Controllers** OU and click **Properties**. If you have worked with Active Directory Users and Computers in Windows Server 2003, you might notice that the Group Policy tab is missing. In Windows Server 2008, all group policy management is done with the Group Policy Management MMC. Click **Cancel**.

11. Click the **Users** folder in the left pane. The right pane displays a list of groups and two user accounts created by default when Active Directory is installed. The Users folder holds these default users, but you should create new users in OUs that you create.

12. Right-click the domain node, point to **New**, and click **Organizational Unit**. In the Name text box, type **OU1**. Uncheck the **Protect container from accidental deletion** check box, and then click **OK**.

13. Make sure **OU1** is selected in the left pane, and then right-click in the right pane, point to **New**, and click **User**.

14. In the First name text box, type **User**, and in the Last name text box, type **One**. Notice that the Full name text box is filled in automatically.

15. In the User logon name text box, type **User1**. The User logon name (pre-Windows 2000) text box is filled in automatically. (A user logon name longer than 20 characters is truncated to 20 characters in this text box.)

16. Click **Next**. In the Password text box, type **mypassword**, and type it again in the Confirm password text box. Note that the "User must change password at next logon" check box is selected by default. Click **Next**, and then click **Finish**.

17. If you get an error message, read it carefully. By default, Windows Server 2008 requires a complex password, meaning the password must be of a minimum length and have at least three of the following types of characters: uppercase letters, lowercase letters, numbers, and special characters. Click **OK**.

18. Click **Back**. In the Password text box, type **Password01**, making sure the P is capitalized and the last two characters are the numerals 0 and 1. Retype the password in the Confirm password text box. Click **Next**, and then click **Finish**.

19. Right-click in the right pane of Active Directory Users and Computers, point to **New**, and click **Group**.

20. Type **Group1G** in the Group name text box (see Figure 3-2). Verify that the Group scope setting is Global and the Group type setting is Security, and then click **OK**.

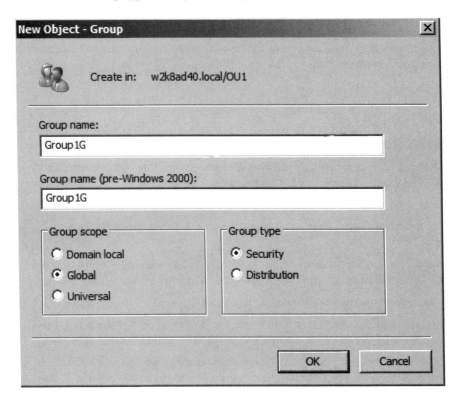

Figure 3-2 Creating a new group

21. Double-click **User One** to open its Properties dialog box.

22. Click the **Member Of** tab. This user account is already a member of the Domain Users group; all new users are members of this group by default.

23. Click the **Add** button to open the Select Groups dialog box. In the Enter the object names to select text box, type **Group1G,** and then click the **Check Names** button. Active Directory verifies that the group name you entered exists and underlines it if it does. If the group doesn't exist, a Name Not Found message box is displayed. In this box, you can correct the group name. Click **OK**, and then click **OK** again. Close all open windows.

Review Questions

1. Which of the following is the graphical tool used to create user and group accounts in Active Directory?

   a. Active Directory Users and Computers

   b. Active Directory Domains and Sites

   c. Active Directory Groups and Users

   d. Active Directory Domains and Trusts

2. _____ is a folder where default user and group accounts are located.

   a. Users

   b. Groups

   c. Builtin

   d. Accounts

3. True or False? By default, Windows Server 2008 allows blank passwords on new accounts created in Active Directory.

4. Which of the following Active Directory containers is an OU?

   a. Computers

   b. Domain Controllers

   c. Users

   d. All of the above

5. What two properties must you verify when creating a new group in Active Directory?

   _____ _____.

Lab 3.3 Using the Command Line and Batch Files to Create Active Directory Objects

Objectives

- Create Active Directory objects using the command line program DSADD
- Modify Active Directory objects using DSMOD
- Create batch files to run DSADD and DSMOD

Materials Required

This lab requires the following:

- Server1XX

Estimated completion time: **20 minutes**

Activity Background

Creating users with Active Directory Users and Computers is easy but involves access to the Windows GUI and several mouse clicks. The command line allows you to do many tasks more quickly in some cases, and Windows has many command-line programs available for creating and managing Active Directory objects. Among them are DSADD and DSMOD. When using these and related commands, you frequently must specify the distinguished name (DN) of the object with which you want to work. A distinguished name includes the name of the object and the path to the object within Active Directory. The DN has this syntax: CN=CommonName,OU=OrganizationalUnit,DC=DomainComponent.

Keep the following in mind when specifying the DN:

- When specifying an OU object, there is no CN= part of the path
- There may be more than one OU= part of the path
- There is a DC= part of the path for each level in the domain name. For example, mydomain.com is specified DC=mydomain,DC=com
- Folders are specified using CN=

Here are a few examples of distinguished names:

- A user named Mike is in the OU named Marketing in domain domainA.local:

  CN=Mike,OU=Marketing,DC=domainA,DC=local

- A user named Julie is in the Users folder in domain domainA.local:

  CN=Julie,CN=Users,DC=domainA,DC=local

Activity

1. Log on to Server1XX as Administrator, if necessary, and open a command prompt window by clicking **Start**, **Command Prompt**.

2. At its simplest, the DSADD command-line program can create a new user by specifying only the distinguished name of the new user. To create a user with the minimal fuss, type **dsadd user "cn=UserA, ou=OU1, dc=W2k8AD1XX, dc=local"** and press **Enter**. Creating a user in this fashion creates the user, but the account is disabled. The account is disabled because no password was specified. A valid password must be specified to create a user that is not disabled by default.

3. To create a new user, at the command prompt, type **dsadd user "cn=User2, ou=OU1, dc=W2k8AD1XX, dc=local" -upn user2@W2k8AD1XX -Samid user2 -fn User -ln Two -pwd Password01 -memberof "cn=Group1G, ou=OU1, dc=W2k8AD1XX, dc=local"** and press **Enter**. If you get any response other than "dsadd succeeded:" check the command you typed for typos and try again.

   This complex command creates a new user named User Two with a logon name of user2 and a password of Password01, places the user in OU1, and makes the user a member of **Group1G**. Close the command prompt window.

4. Open Active Directory Users and Computers, and click **OU1** in the left pane if necessary. Verify that User2 is there. Double-click **Group1G**, and then click the **Members** tab to verify that this new user is a member. Click **OK**.

5. The dsadd command is syntax-intensive and typos are common. If you will likely be creating users using the command-line, a batch file is recommended. Notepad is a fine tool for creating batch files. Click **Start** and type **notepad** in the Start Search box and press **Enter**.

6. Type **dsadd user "cn=%3,ou=%4,dc=W2k8AD1XX,dc=local" -upn %3@W2k8AD1XX -Samid %3 -fn %1 -ln %2 -pwd Password01**. (Note that the period at the end of the previous sentence is not part of the command.)

7. Save the file in your Documents folder. Click **File** and click **Save As**. In the Save as type box, click the list arrow and click **All Files**. In the File name box, type **Uadd.bat** and click **Save**. Close Notepad.

8. When you run the Uadd.bat file, the %1, %2, %3, and %4 will be replaced by command line arguments you supply. Open a command prompt, if necessary. Go to the Documents directory: type **cd documents** and press **Enter**. Type **Uadd User Three User3 OU1** and press **Enter**. This command creates a new user with a first and last name of User Three; the logon name will be User3 in OU1.

9. Return to Active Directory Users and Computer to see that the user has been created.

10. Similarly, you can create a batch file that adds a user to a group. Open Notepad and type the following command: **dsmod group "cn=%2,ou=%3,dc=W2k8AD1XX,dc=local" -addmbr "cn=%1,ou=%3, dc=W2k8AD1XX,dc=local"**. (Note that the period at the end of the previous sentence is not part of the command.) Save the file as AddtoGroup.bat in the Documents folder.

11. At the command prompt, type **AddtoGroup User3 Group1G OU1** and press **Enter**. This command will add User3 to Group1G in OU1. Note that if you will be adding users located in a different OU than your group, you will need an additional %x argument specification in the batch file.

12. In Active Directory Users and Computers double-click **Group1G** and click the **Members** tab to verify that User3 has been successfully added.

13. Close all open windows. If you are going on to the next lab, stay logged on to Server1XX. Otherwise, log off Server1XX.

Review Questions

1. Which of the following must be specified to create a user using DSADD User?

   a. The common name

   b. The distinguished name

   c. The common name and the password

   d. The distinguished name and the password

2. The correct DN syntax to specify a user named Sharon, in the Sales OU, which is in the Marketing OU, in domain mydomain.local is _____.

   a. cn=Sharon,OU=Marketing,OU=Sales,DC=mydomain.local

   b. cn=Sharon,OU=Marketing,OU=Sales,DC=mydomain,DC=local

   c. cn=Sharon,OU=Sales,OU=Marketing,DC=mydomain.local

   d. cn=Sharon,OU=Sales,OU=Marketing,DC=mydomain,DC=local

3. True or False? To add an existing user to an existing group, you can use the dsmod group command.

4. Which of the following is the correct syntax to specify a parameter in a batch file?

   a. $x

   b. %x

   c. &x

   d. @x

5. Using the batch file you created in this lab, write the command you would type to do the following: add user Doris to group Execs where both Doris and Execs are existing objects in OU Admin in domain W2k8AD1XX.local?

   _____

Lab 3.4 Create, Publish, and Find a Shared Folder in Active Directory

Objectives

- Create a Shared folder using Advanced Sharing
- Publish a shared folder in Active Directory
- Use Windows Explorer to search for Active Directory objects

Materials Required

This lab requires the following:

- Server1XX

Estimated completion time: **20 minutes**

Activity Background

In a network with dozens or even just several servers, it can be difficult for users to keep up with which server hosts which shared folder. The ability to publish shares in Active Directory and allow users to search for shares from the Windows Explorer interface alleviates some of that difficulty.

Activity

1. Log on to your server as Administrator, if necessary.

2. Click **Start**, **Computer**. Double-click the **C** drive to open a Windows Explorer window.

3. Create a new folder in the root of the C drive by right-clicking an empty space in the right pane, pointing to **New,** and clicking **Folder.** Type **PublishedShare** for the name of the new folder and press **Enter.**

4. Right-click **PublishedShare** and click **Properties.** Click the **Sharing** tab.

5. On the Sharing tab, click the **Advanced Sharing** button. Click **Share this folder.** Click **OK.**

6. Click **Close** on the Sharing tab.

7. Click **Start,** point to **Administrative Tools,** and click **Computer Management.**

8. Click to expand the **Shared Folders** node, and then click the **Shares** folder.

9. In the right pane, double-click **PublishedShare** to open its Properties dialog box.

10. Click the **Publish** tab (see Figure 3-3), and then check the **Publish this share in Active Directory** check box.

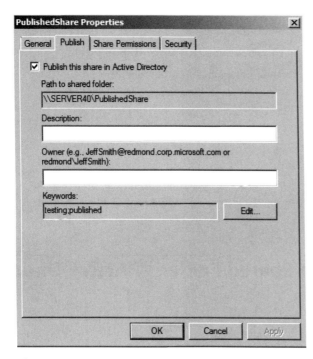

Figure 3-3   The Publish tab of a shared folder's Properties dialog box

11. In the Description text box, type **A shared folder that is published in Active Directory.**

12. Click the **Edit** button. In the Edit Keywords dialog box, type **published,** and then click **Add.** Type **testing** and then click **Add.** Click **OK** twice.

13. Close all open windows. Click **Start, Network.**

14. Click the **Search Active Directory** toolbar button.

15. In the Find drop-down list, click **Shared Folders.**

16. In the Keywords text box, type **publish,** and then click **Find Now.**

17. In the Search results section, right-click **PublishedShare** and click **Explore.** A Windows Explorer window opens, showing the contents of the PublishedShare shared folder (currently empty).

18. Close all open windows.

19. Open Active Directory Users and Computers.

20. When you publish a shared folder by using Computer Management, the published share appears as a child object of the server on which the share is located. To view child objects of servers, click **View, Users, Contacts, Groups,** and **Computers as containers** from the menu.

21. Click to expand the **Domain Controllers** OU, and then click the **server** icon. You should see the share you published in the right pane (see Figure 3-4).

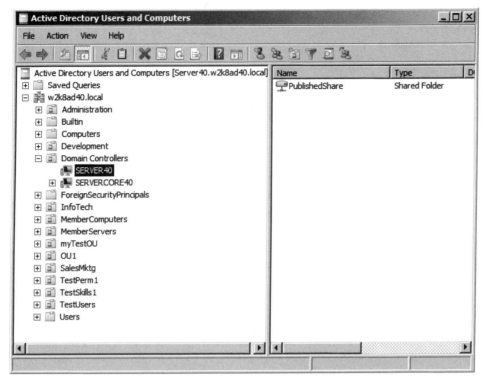

Figure 3-4   A published share in Active Directory Users and Computers

22. Click **View, Users, Contacts, Groups,** and **Computers as containers** from the menu again to disable this feature, and then close Active Directory Users and Computers. If you are going on to the next lab, stay logged on to Server1XX. Otherwise, log off Server XX.

Review Questions

1. True or False? You can publish a share using the Shared Folders snap-in in the Computer Management MMC.

2. Which of the following can you do from the Advanced Sharing dialog box? (Choose all that apply.)

   a. Share a folder

   b. Limit the number of simultaneous users

   c. Publish a folder in Active Directory

   d. Name the share

3. True or False? Users can view published shares in Active Directory, but they cannot browse the shares.

4. After you click the Search Active Directory button, you have the option to search based on which of the following criteria? (Choose all that apply.)

   a. Type of object

   b. Where in the directory to search

   c. Name of the object

   d. Date the object was created

5. True or False? To bring up a Windows Explorer window that includes the Search Active Directory icon, click Start and then Computer.

Lab 3.5 Browsing and Using Group Policies

Objectives

- Use Group Policy Management Console and Group Policy Management Editor
- Explore the major policy nodes
- Create policies to affect a user's working environment

Materials Required

This lab requires the following:

- Server1XX

Estimated completion time: **20 minutes**

Activity Background

One of the most powerful aspects of Active Directory is Group Policy. The Group Policy Management Console provides an administrator with a tool to organize and monitor group policy objects (GPOs). The Group Policy Management Editor lets administrators modify and create new group policies. There are two primary nodes in every GPO: Computer Configuration and User Configuration. Hundreds of policies reside within each node. There are two default GPOs: the Default Domain Policy and the Default Domain Controllers Policy. The Default Domain Policy is linked to the domain object and affects all objects in the domain whereas the Default Domain Controllers Policy is linked to the Domain Controllers OU and affects domain controllers only.

Activity

1. Log on to Server1XX as Administrator, if necessary.

2. Click **Start**, point to **Administrative Tools**, and click **Group Policy Management**.

3. In the left pane, double-click to expand the **Forest** and **Domains** nodes, if necessary.

4. Double-click to expand your domain name under the Domains node, if necessary. You should see a window similar to Figure 3-5.

5. Click **Default Domain Policy**. If a Group Policy Management Console message appears, read the message, click the **Do not show this message again** check box, and then click **OK**.

6. In the right pane, click the **Scope** tab, if necessary. The Links section shows you which container objects are linked to this GPO. In this case, your domain should be the only container linked. All objects in a container linked to the GPO are affected by that GPO.

7. Click the **Settings** tab, as shown in Figure 3-6. (The settings might take a few seconds to be displayed.) You can view GPO settings here, but you can't change them.

8. Two primary nodes are highlighted: Computer Configuration and User Configuration. Click the **show all** link to expand the settings.

9. Scroll through the settings for the Default Domain Policy, which pertain to user account settings, such as password policies or security. Note that no settings are displayed under the User Configuration node.

10. Double-click **Domain Controllers** in the left pane, and then click **Default Domain Controllers Policy**. You can view the settings and other information for this GPO just as you did for the Default Domain Policy.

11. Right-click **Default Domain Controllers Policy** in the left pane and click **Edit**. The Group Policy Management Editor opens.

12. Under Computer Configuration, click to expand **Policies** and **Windows Settings**, and then click to expand the **Security Settings** node.

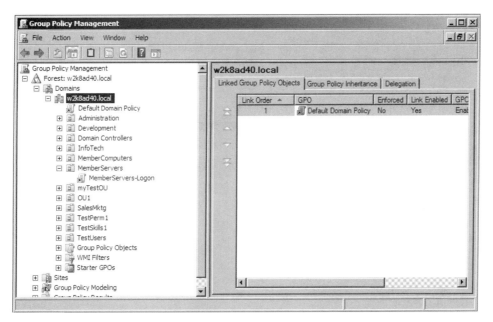

Figure 3-5   Group Policy Management Console

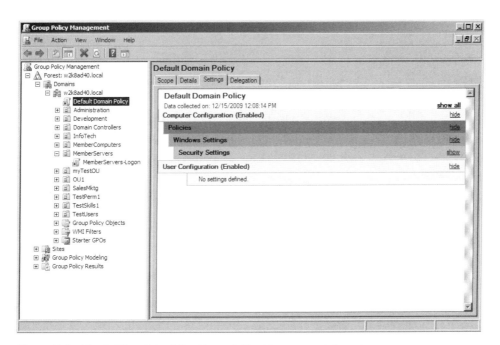

Figure 3-6   The Settings tab of the Group Policy Management Console

13. Click to expand **Local Policies**, and then click **User Rights Assignment**. You should see a list of User Rights Assignment policies in the right pane (see Figure 3-7).

14. In the right pane, double-click the **Allow log on locally** policy. By default, only members of the groups listed in the policy can log on to a domain controller. Click **Add User or Group**. In the Add User or Group dialog box, type **Domain Users**, and then click **OK** twice. This will allow new users you create to log on to the Server1XX domain controller.

15. Close all open windows. To test this policy, you will log on as the User1 that you created earlier. However, it can take a few minutes for the policy change to take effect. To apply the policy immediately, open a command prompt and type **gpupdate** and press **Enter**. Gpupdate causes changed group policies to be applied immediately to the computer on which it is run.

16. Switch user by clicking **Start**, pointing to the arrow next to the padlock icon, and clicking **Switch User**.

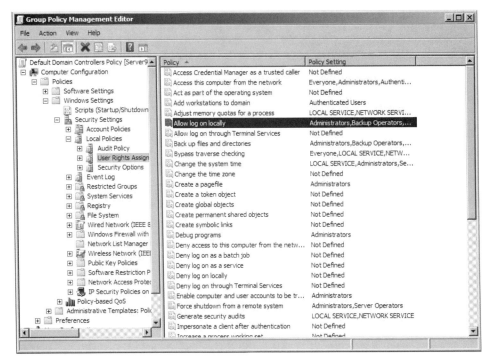

Figure 3-7   User Rights Assignments policies

17. Press **Ctrl+Alt+Delete** and click **Other User**. Type **user1** in the User name text box and **Password01** in the Password text box and then click the arrow.

18. In the message stating that the user's password must be changed before logging on the first time, click **OK**.

19. In the New Password text box, type **Password02**, and then type it again in the Confirm password text box. Click the arrow to log on. Click **OK** when you get the message that the password has been changed.

20. Click **Start**, right-click **Computer,** and click **Show on Desktop**.

21. Right-click your desktop and click **Personalize**. Click **Screen Saver**. Click the up arrow next to the **Wait** box until the number in the box is 15. Click **OK**.

22. Log off Server1XX and log back on as Administrator.

23. Click **Start**, point to **Administrative Tools,** and click **Group Policy Management**.

24. Click to expand the **Forest** and **Domains** nodes and then your domain node, if necessary.

25. Right-click **OU1** (created earlier) and click **Create a GPO in this domain, and Link it here**.

26. In the New GPO dialog box, type **OU1GPO** in the Name text box, and then click **OK**.

27. In the left pane, click **OU1** and then in the right pane, right-click the **OU1GPO** you just created and click **Edit** to open the Group Policy Management Editor.

28. Under User Configuration, click to expand **Policies** and then **Administrative Templates**.

29. Click to expand the **Control Panel** node. Click **Display**. In the right pane, double-click **Screen Saver timeout**.

30. In the Screen Saver timeout Properties dialog, click the **Enabled** option button. In the Seconds box, type **1800**. Click **OK**. This sets the screen saver timeout from 15 minutes to 30 minutes.

31. In the left pane of Group Policy Management Editor, click **Desktop**. In the right pane, double-click **Remove Computer icon on the desktop** and click the **Enabled** option button. Click **OK**.

32. Close all open windows.

33. Log on as **User1** and see if the policies have taken effect. The Computer icon should not be on the desktop. Right-click your desktop and click **Personalize**. Click **Screen Saver**. You should see that the number in the Wait box is 30, and it is grayed out indicating that you cannot change it. When a setting is set through Group Policy, users cannot change the setting.

34. Log off and log back on as Administrator.

35. Open **Group Policy Management Console**. To unlink OU1GPO from OU1, click to expand **OU1**. Right-click **OU1GPO** and click **Delete**. Click **OK** when asked if you want to delete the link. Users in OU1 will no longer be subject to the policies set in OU1GPO.

36. If you are going on to the next chapter's labs, stay logged on to Server1XX. Otherwise, shut down Server1XX.

3

Review Questions

1. The primary nodes in every GPO are _____ nodes. (Choose all that apply.)

   a. Group Configuration

   b. Computer Configuration

   c. User Configuration

   d. Domain Controller Configuration

2. A policy set in the Default Domain Controllers GPO typically affects all _____ in the domain.

   a. users

   b. domain controllers

   c. computers

   d. servers

3. User Rights Assignment policies are found under the _____ primary GPO node.

4. True or False? Group policy changes immediately affect the objects in their scope.

5. True or False? Domain users can log on to a domain controller by default.

ACTIVE DIRECTORY DESIGN AND SECURITY CONCEPTS

Labs included in this chapter

- Lab 4.1 Creating OUs and Delegating Control
- Lab 4.2 Working with Active Directory Permissions from the Command Line
- Lab 4.3 Browsing the Schema and Determining Operations Masters
- Lab 4.4 Exploring and Configuring Sites

Microsoft MCTS Exam #70-640 Objectives

Objective	Lab
Creating and Maintaining Active Directory Objects	4.1, 4.2
Configuring the Active Directory Infrastructure	4.3, 4.4

Lab 4.1 Creating OUs and Delegating Control

Objectives

- Create organizational units
- Work with delegation of control and Active Directory object permissions

Materials Required

This lab requires the following:

- Server1XX

Estimated completion time: **15 minutes**

Activity Background

OUs are the primary organizing container to manage Active Directory objects in a domain. To properly organize Active Directory objects, a well-designed OU structure is paramount.

Server administrators spend a great deal of time working with Active Directory objects. Objects need to be renamed, group memberships need to be updated, passwords must be reset, and so forth. In a large network, an administrator can become overwhelmed with the tasks such that it might be tempting to grant junior IT technicians administrator group membership so that they can share the load. However, a more secure solution exists. Administrators can delegate control of many tasks to certain parts of the Active Directory structure, thus allowing junior IT technicians the ability to do tasks such as reset passwords and modify group memberships but not delete objects. In addition, the delegation can be restricted to objects within a single OU, if necessary, giving you fine-grained control over the objects to which users have access.

Activity

1. Log on to Server1XX as Administrator, if necessary.

2. Click **Start**, point to **Administrative Tools**, and click **Active Directory Users and Computers**.

3. Right-click the domain node **W2k8AD1XX.local**, point to **New**, and click **Organizational Unit**.

4. In the Name text box, type **Administration**. Check the **Protect container from accidental deletion** check box, if necessary, and then click **OK**.

> If you need to delete or move an OU, you will need to uncheck the Protect container from accidental deletion check box. This check box can be found on the Object tab of an OU's properties.

5. Repeat Steps 3 and 4 to create the SalesMktg, Development, and InfoTech OUs. When finished, your OU structure should be similar to Figure 4-1.

6. Right-click the **InfoTech** OU, point to **New**, and click **User**.

7. Type **Mike** in the First name text box, **NewTech** in the Last name text box, and **MNewTech** in the User logon name text box. Click **Next**.

8. Type **Password01** in the Password text box and again in the Confirm password text box. Uncheck the **User must change password at next logon** check box, click **Next**, and then click **Finish**.

9. Right-click the **Development** OU and click **Delegate Control** to start the Delegation of Control Wizard. Click **Next**.

10. Click **Add**. In the Enter the object names to select text box, type **MNewTech**. Click **Check Names**, and then click **OK**. Click **Next**.

11. Check the **Reset user passwords and force password change at next logon** check box. Click **Next**, and then click **Finish**.

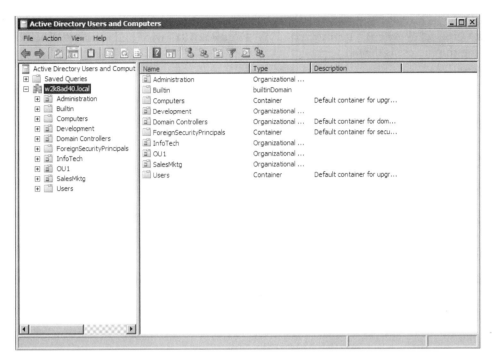

Figure 4-1   An OU structure in Active Directory Users and Computers

12. Click **View, Advanced Features** from the menu, and verify that Advanced Features is selected with a check mark. Right-click the **Development** OU and click **Properties**. The Advanced Features option gives you access to three additional properties tabs of Active Directory objects: Object, Security, and Attribute Editor. Click the **Security** tab. Click the **Mike NewTech** ACE, and scroll the permissions list at the bottom. Note that only the Allow Special permissions check box is selected.

13. Click the **Advanced** button to open the Advanced Security Settings for Development dialog box.

14. Double-click the first **Mike NewTech** entry. The Reset password check box is selected in the Allow column, so Mike NewTech has permission to reset user's passwords in the Development OU. The "Descendant User objects" option in the Apply to list means Mike NewTech can reset user passwords in the Development OU and any OUs under the Development OU. Click **Cancel**.

15. Double-click the second **Mike NewTech** entry. You will find that the Read pwdLastSet and Write pwd-LastSet permissions are allowed. If you were to create a customized delegation of control, you would need to know which permissions were required to allow specific actions to be performed.

16. Click **Cancel** until only the Active Directory Users and Computers window is open.

17. Click the **Development** OU and click the **Create a new user** icon in the toolbar. Type **Dev** in the First name box and **User1** in the Last name box. Type **DevUser1** in the User logon name box. Click **Next**.

18. Type **Password01** in the Password and Confirm password boxes. Click **Next**. Click **Finish**.

19. Log off Server1XX and log on Server1XX as **MNewTech**. Open **Active Directory Users and Computers**. User Account Control will prompt you for MNewTech's password. Type **Password01** and click **OK**.

20. In Active Directory Users and Computers, click to expand **W2k8AD1XX.local** and click the **Development** OU. Notice that the Create a new user icon in the toolbar is grayed out. Double-click **Dev User1**. Browse the properties of **Dev User1.** Notice that you can view the properties of the user but that you cannot change them.

21. Click the **Account** tab. Notice that the only Account option that is not grayed out is the User must change password at next logon option. Click **Cancel**.

22. Right-click **Dev User1** and click **Disable Account**. You get a message stating that you have insufficient rights to perform the operation. Click **OK**.

23. Right-click **Dev User1** and click **Reset Password**. Type **Password02** twice. Click **OK**. Click **OK** on the message indicating the password has been changed. As you can see, the user MNewTech can view user's properties in the Development OU but cannot change any values except the properties related to the password.

24. To verify that MNewTech only has password-changing privileges in the Development OU, click **OU1** and right-click **User One**. Click **Reset Password**. Type **Password$!** twice and click **OK**. Click **OK** on the message indicating that access is denied.

25. Log off Server1XX.

Review Questions

1. True or False? By default, new OUs are protected from accidental deletion.

2. Which of the following is *not* a task set that you can delegate using the Delegation of Control Wizard?

   a. Create, delete, and manage groups

   b. Create, delete, and manage OUs

   c. Modify the membership of a group

   d. Read all user information

3. When the Delegation of Control Wizard is used to delegate the Reset password permission, which of the following is the default inheritance setting for the permission?

   a. Descendant User objects

   b. This object only

   c. All descendant objects

   d. This object and all descendant objects

4. True or False? When a user has been delegated control to an object, he or she automatically is made a member of the Server Operators group.

5. The user attribute that pertains to the User must change password at next logon account option is _____.

Lab 4.2 Working with Active Directory Permissions from the Command Line

Objectives

- Download and use the dsrevoke command
- Use the dsacls command

Materials Required

This lab requires the following:

- Server1XX

Estimated completion time: **10 minutes**

Activity Background

If you can create and modify objects from the command line, it follows that you should be able to manage object permissions. Dsacls is the command-line program included with Windows Server 2008 to do just that. Like most of the ds command-line programs, batch files are probably the way to go with dsacls. Dsrevoke is a simpler command-line program that you can download from the Microsoft download site. Dsrevoke provides similar functionality to Dsacls but is easier to use when you wish to remove permissions. This lab introduces you to these two command-line programs so that you can set Active Directory object permissions without the GUI.

Activity

1. If necessary, log on to Server1XX as Administrator.

2. To download the command-line program DSREVOKE.EXE, open Internet Explorer. Type **www. Microsoft.com/downloads** in the Address bar and click **Go**. In the Search All Download Center box, type **dsrevoke.exe** and press **Enter**.

3. Click **DSREVOKE.EXE** in the results. On the DESREVOKE.EXE page, scroll down until you see the Download button. Click the **Download** button next to dsrevoke.exe. Click **Save**.

4. In the Save As dialog, click **Browse Folders**. Click **Computer** and double-click the **C:** drive. Double-click **Windows** and click **Save**. In the Download complete message, click **Close**.

must be in this location

5. Open a command prompt. Type **dsrevoke /report W2k8AD1XX\MNewTech | more** and press **Enter**. You see a list of the ACEs for MNewTech. Press **Spacebar** to page through the rest of the output.

6. To remove MNewTech from the permissions lists shown in the previous step, type **dsrevoke /remove W2k8AD1XX\MNewTech** and press **Enter**. You are prompted to remove the ACEs listed in Step 5. Press **y** and press **Enter**.

7. Open Active Directory Users and Computers. Right-click the **Development** OU and click **Properties**. Click the **Security** tab and verify that Mike NewTech is no longer in the list of ACEs. Click **Cancel** to close the Development Properties dialog box.

8. The DSACLS command lets you set permissions using the command line. The syntax is somewhat complex and is another command that you might want to implement as a batch file. At the command prompt, type **dsacls ou=development,dc=W2k8AD1XX,dc=local /g W2k8AD1XX\mnewtech:GA** and press **Enter**. That command gives Mike NewTech all permissions to the Development OU. The GA at the end of the command means Generic All. For help on using DSACLS, type **DSACLS | more** and press **Enter**. Press **Spacebar** to page through the output until you see the command prompt.

9. Return to Active Directory Users and Computers. Right-click the **Development** OU and click **Properties**. Click the **Security** tab to see that Mike NewTech is now listed and has the Allow permission for each permission type. Click **Cancel** to close the Development Properties dialog box.

10. At this point, you can use DSREVOKE to remove Mike NewTech from the permissions list. To do so, repeat Step 6 in this lab.

11. Remain logged on to Server1XX if you are continuing to the next lab. Otherwise, log off Server1XX.

Review Questions

1. True or False? DSREVOKE.EXE comes standard with Windows Server 2008.

2. What option should you supply DSACLS when you want to allow a specified permission?

   a. /G

   b. /A

   c. /P

   d. /D

3. Which of the following commands would remove user sjohnson from the DACL all Active Directory objects in domain W2k8AD1XX?

   a. dsrevoke /report W2k8AD1XX\sjohnson

   b. dsacls /deny W2k8AD1XX\sjohnson

   c. dsrevoke /remove W2k8AD1XX\sjohnson

   d. dsacls /D W2k8AD1XX\sjohnson /all

4. True or False? The DSACLS command can be used only to change permissions, not view them.

5. Write the command that would deny all permissions to the Operations OU to a user in the W2k8AD1XX. local domain named bsmith. _____.

Lab 4.3 Browsing the Schema and Determining Operations Masters

Objectives

- Use the appropriate Active Directory graphical tools to view which domain controllers hold the operations master roles
- Use the Active Directory Schema snap-in to view who holds the schema master role and to view attribute properties
- Use command-line tools to determine what operations masters are held by a domain controller

Materials Required

This lab requires the following:

- Server1XX

Estimated completion time: **20 minutes**

Activity Background

The operations masters are domain controllers that perform key functions to ensure proper operation of Active Directory. The functions provided are referred to as flexible single master operations (FSMO) role. There are five FSMO roles: schema master, domain naming master, infrastructure master, PDC emulator, and RID master. The schema master and domain naming master are forest-wide roles and are found only on domain controllers in the forest root domain. The other three FSMO roles are domain-wide functions and reside on one domain controller in each domain. It is critical that an administrator know by which domain controllers each of the FSMO roles is held.

The schema holds a list of all object classes and attributes in Active Directory. The Active Directory Schema snap-in lets you view and change the properties of schema objects and attributes. You know that the Global Catalog holds a partial replica of Active Directory attributes, which means that some attributes are held in the Global Catalog and others are not. You can view and change which attributes are copied to the Global Catalog using the Active Directory Schema snap-in.

Activity

1. Log on to Server1XX as Administrator, if necessary, and open Active Directory Users and Computers.

2. Right-click **Active Directory Users and Computers [Server1XX.W2k8AD1XX.local]**, point to **All Tasks**, and click **Operations Masters**.

3. The RID tab shows which domain controller performs the RID master role. Click the **Change** button. The error message tells you that the DC to which you're connected is the operations master, and you must first connect to the domain controller to which you want to transfer the operations master role. Click **OK**.

4. Click the **PDC** tab to view the DC that's the PDC emulator master. Click the **Infrastructure** tab to view the DC that's the infrastructure master. These operations master roles are performed by only one DC per domain. Click **Close**.

5. Right-click **Active Directory Users and Computers [Server1XX.W2k8AD1XX.local]** and click **Change Domain Controller**. If your domain had more than one DC, you could connect to any of them here and then change the operations master role to the chosen DC. Click **Cancel**. Close Active Directory Users and Computers.

6. Click **Start**, point to **Administrative Tools**, and click **Active Directory Domains and Trusts**.

7. Right-click **Active Directory Domains and Trusts [Server1XX.W2k8AD1XX.local]** and click **Operations Master**. Here's where you can find which DC is the domain naming master. Note that only one DC in the forest performs this function and it is always on the first domain controller installed in the first domain in the forest. Click **Close**. Close Active Directory Domains and Trusts.

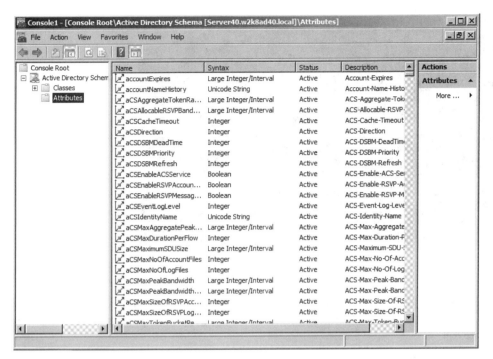

Figure 4-2   Active Directory Schema snap-in

8. To view the schema master, you must use a different process because this role isn't shown in any of the standard MMCs. Click **Start, Run**, type **regsvr32 schmmgmt.dll** in the Open text box, and click **OK**. In the message box stating that DllRegisterServer in schmmgmt.dll succeeded, click **OK**.

> The regsvr32 command is necessary to register, or activate, certain commands that aren't normally available in Windows—in this case, the Active Directory Schema snap-in.

9. Click **Start, Run**, type **MMC** in the Open text box, and click **OK**.

10. Click **File, Add/Remove Snap-in** from the MMC menu.

11. In the Available snap-ins list box, click **Active Directory Schema**. Click **Add**, and then click **OK**.

12. Click to select **Active Directory Schema**, then right-click **Active Directory Schema** and click **Operations Master**. Note that only one DC in the entire forest performs the schema master role. Click **Close**.

13. Click to expand the **Active Directory Schema** node if necessary and click **Attributes**. A list of object attributes is displayed in the right pane (see Figure 4-2).

14. Scroll through the attributes until you find userPassword (the attributes are listed in alphabetical order). Double-click **userPassword**. Examine the check boxes. The Replicate this attribute to the Global Catalog check box is not checked, so this attribute is not copied to the Global Catalog. Click **Cancel**.

15. Double-click the **userPrincipalName** attribute. Because the user principal name is a likely field on which to search for users, it is copied to the Global Catalog. Click **Cancel**.

16. In the Active Directory Schema console, click **File** and click **Save As**. The default location to save a custom MMC is in Administrative Tools. Type **Schema Management** in the File name box and click **Save**. You will use this MMC again in Lab 5.2. Close Schema Management.

17. Open a command prompt if necessary. Type **ntdsutil** and press **Enter**. Ntdsutil is a command-line interactive utility for managing the Active Directory database.

18. Type **roles** and press **Enter**. The prompt changes to fsmo maintenance. At any prompt, you can type a question mark to see the possible commands you can enter. Type **?** and press **Enter**. A list of possible commands for fsmo maintenance is displayed (see Figure 4-3). Note that most of the commands start with Seize or Transfer. Seizing and Transferring roles are discussed in Chapter 10.

Figure 4-3 The NTDSUTIL command and possible commands for fsmo maintenance

19. Type **connections** and press **Enter**. You can connect to a domain controller from this prompt. Type **connect to server Server1XX** and press **Enter**. Type **quit** and press **Enter** to leave the server connections context.

20. Type **select operation target** and press **Enter**. Type **list roles for connected server** and press **Enter**. Because this server is the only domain controller, it holds all five FSMO roles.

21. Type **quit** followed by **Enter** three times to exit ntdsutil. Close all open windows. Stay logged on to Server1XX if you are continuing to the next lab. Otherwise, log off Server1XX.

Review Questions

1. Which of the following FSMO roles is a forest-wide role? (Choose all that apply.)

   a. Schema master

   b. RID master

   c. Domain naming master

   d. PDC emulator

   e. Infrastructure master

2. Which of the following FSMO roles can you view using Active Directory Users and Computers? (Choose all that apply.)

   a. Schema master

   b. RID master

   c. Domain naming master

   d. PDC emulator

   e. Infrastructure master

3. Which of the following FSMO roles requires the registration of a dll file to manage it?

   a. Schema master

   b. RID master

   c. Domain naming master

   d. PDC emulator

   e. Infrastructure master

4. True or False? The regsvr32 command is used to manage the Active Directory database.

5. You can change which attributes are copied to the Global Catalog by using the _____ snap-in.

Lab 4.4 Exploring and Configuring Sites

Objectives

- Explore Active Directory Sites and Services MMC
- Rename the default site name to a more descriptive name
- Create a new subnet and associate it with your site

4

Materials Required

This lab requires the following:

- Server1XX

Estimated completion time: **10 minutes**

Activity Background

Sites are one of the physical components of the Active Directory structure. Sites are associated with one or more IP subnets and contain domain controllers whose IP addresses reside in the associated subnet. You can create new subnets, associate subnets to sites, create new sites, and change replication options between sites using Active Directory Sites and Services. Other Active Directory objects you can manage here include bridgehead servers, connection objects, and site links. This lab introduces sites and the Active Directory Sites and Services MMC.

Activity

1. Log on to Server1XX as Administrator, if necessary.

2. Click **Start**, point to **Administrative Tools**, and click **Active Directory Sites and Services**.

3. Click to expand **Sites**, if necessary. Click to expand **Default-First-Site-Name** and click to expand **Servers**. The Servers folder in a site folder contains the domain controllers that have been assigned to the site. In this case, you should see Server1XX.

4. Click **Server1XX** and in the right pane, right-click **NTDS Settings** and click **Properties**. The check box on the General tab allows you to change whether the server holds a copy of the Global Catalog.

5. Click the **Connections** tab. If you had more than one domain controller, you would see a list of this DC's replication partners in the Replicate From and Replicate To boxes. Click **Cancel**.

6. Click to expand **Inter-Site Transports**. Click the **IP** folder. In the right pane you see an object named DEFAULTIPSITELINK. Right-click **DEFAULTIPSITELINK** and click **Properties**. On the General tab (see Figure 4-4), you can view and change the site link cost and replication schedule between sites that use this link. Right now, you only have one site. Click **Cancel**.

7. Right-click **Default-First-Site-Name** and click **Rename**. It's always a good idea to use a descriptive name for your site, even when you only have one. Type **SiteXX-Subnet100**. Next you will create a new subnet and associate it with SiteXX-Subnet100.

8. Right-click **Subnets** and click **New Subnet**.

9. In the Prefix text box, type **192.168.100.0/24** (this address assumes you're following the IP address scheme used in this book; if you are not following this IP address scheme, ask your instructor what to enter).

10. In the Select a site object for this prefix list box, click **SiteXX-Subnet100**, and then click **OK**. This associates SiteXX-Subnet100 with the 192.168.100.0/24 subnet.

11. In the left pane, click **Subnets**. Right-click **192.168.100.0/24** and click **Properties**. In the General tab, you can give the subnet a description and change the site with which the subnet is associated.

12. Click **Cancel**. Close Active Directory Sites and Services. Log off and shut down Server1XX.

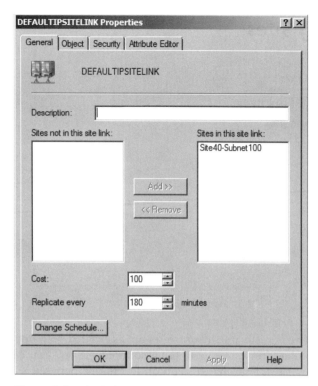

Figure 4-4   Site link properties

Review Questions

1. Which of the following are considered physical components of the Active Directory structure? (Choose all that apply.)

   a. Domains

   b. Sites

   c. OUs

   d. Domain Controllers

   e. Forests

2. Which component of a site should you modify if you want to change the replication schedule between sites?

   a. Subnet

   b. Connection

   c. Site link

   d. Server

3. Which of the following is a valid prefix value?

   a. 150

   b. 149.18:16

   c. 192.168.110.0[20]

   d. 150.11.0.0/16

4. True or False? You cannot change the name of the first site, which is created automatically.

5. The name of the IP site link that is automatically created is _____ .

CHAPTER FIVE

ACCOUNT MANAGEMENT

Labs included in this chapter

- Lab 5.1 Install Windows PowerShell and Create New Users
- Lab 5.2 Create User Templates and Change Schema Attribute Properties
- Lab 5.3 Setting Logon Hours and Logon Station
- Lab 5.4 Change Default Computer Location and Add a Client Computer Account to the Domain

Microsoft MCTS Exam #70-640 Objectives

Objective	Lab
Creating and Maintaining Active Directory Objects	5.1, 5.2, 5.3, 5.4

Lab 5.1 Install Windows PowerShell and Create New Users

Objectives

- Install Windows PowerShell
- Create Users with Windows PowerShell

Materials Required

This lab requires the following:

- Server1XX

Estimated completion time: **15 minutes**

Activity Background

Windows PowerShell is a powerful new scripting language available in Windows. PowerShell provides a command-line interface that gives you access to many features and functions, including Active Directory management features. In most cases, you will not use PowerShell interactively except to test and refine script commands. Instead, you will create script files that can be run to execute a series of PowerShell commands to perform a particular function; this process is similar to using batch files for DSADD and other commands.

The following activity introduces you to using PowerShell interactively to test and refine commands. Typically, once you have perfected a series of commands, you would put them into a script file (a text file you can create with Notepad) and either execute them from within the PowerShell command or execute the PowerShell command followed by the script file name. For example, if your script is named c:\scripts\CreateUsers.ps1 (ps1 is the standard file extension name for a PowerShell version 1 script file, you could execute it by typing PowerShell c:\scripts\CreateUsers.ps1.

Activity

1. Log on to Server1XX as Administrator.

2. Start Server Manager. In the left pane, click **Features**.

3. In the right pane, click **Add Features**.

4. In the Select Features dialog, scroll down until you see Windows PowerShell and then check the **Windows PowerShell** check box. Click **Next**, and then click **Install**.

5. When installation completes, click **Close**.

6. Click **Start**, click **All Programs**, **Windows PowerShell 1.0** and then click **Windows PowerShell**. The Windows PowerShell command prompt opens. The PowerShell command prompt looks almost like a regular command prompt except that the background is blue and the prompt is preceded by the letters PS.

7. PowerShell commands tend to be syntax-intensive, but they are not case sensitive—upper and lower case is used to improve readability. First, we must connect to the domain. Type **$domain_ =_ New-Object_ System.DirectoryServices.DirectoryEntry** and press **Enter**.

8. The command in Step 7 places the domain name in distinguished name format into the variable $domain. To view the contents of the variable, type **$domain,** and press **Enter**. You can list all of the next-level objects under the domain. Type **$domain.psbase.children** and press **Enter**. Figure 5-1 shows the command and the output of the command.

9. Next, you will create a new OU called myTestOU. Type **$newOU_ _ =_ _$domain.Create ("OrganizationalUnit","ou=myTestOU")** and press **Enter**. Next, type **$newOU.Setinfo()** and press **Enter**. The last command creates or commits changes to the object in Active Directory.

10. To confirm the creation of the new OU, type **$domain.psbase.children** and press **Enter**. The new OU, myTestOU, should be displayed in the list of objects.

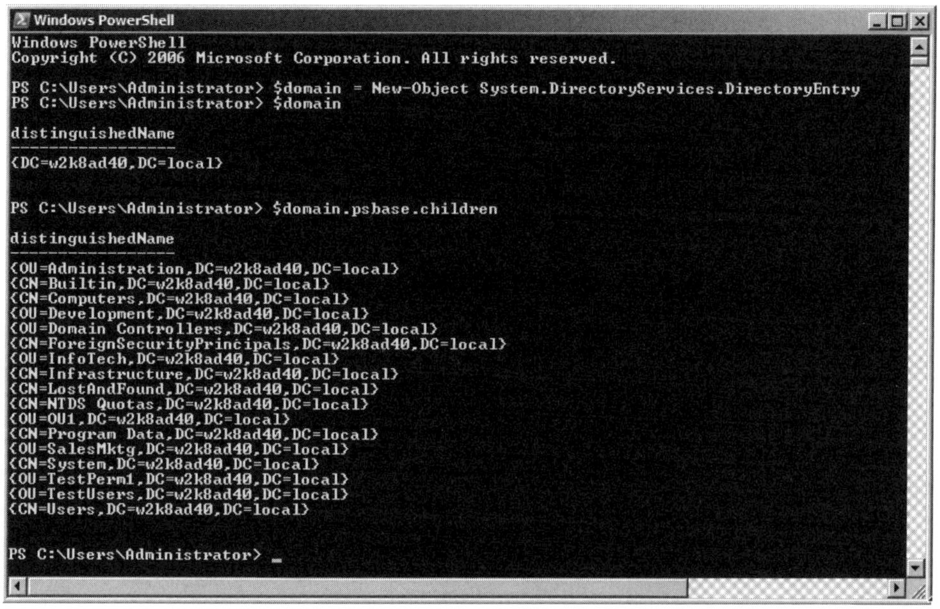

Figure 5-1 PowerShell Active Directory commands

✳ 11. Next, you will create a user in myTestOU. Type `$newUser=$newOU.Create("User","cn=myTestUser1")` and press **Enter**. Type `$newUser.Setinfo()` and press **Enter** to commit the changes.

12. The command in Step 11 sets only the user's distinguished name. Neither the password nor any other attributes are set. The user is created but its state is disabled. Confirm the user is created by typing `$newOU.psbase.children` and pressing **Enter**. That command lists the objects contained in the myTestOU.

13. To complete the creation of a user account, you must set additional attributes. Type `$newUser.SamAccountName __=__"myTestUser1"` and press **Enter**. Type `$newUser.userPrincipalName_ = _"myTestUser1@W2k8AD1XX.local"` and press **Enter**. Type `$newUser.SetPassword("Password01")`, press **Enter**, type `$newUser.SetInfo()`, and press **Enter**.

14. List the attributes of the user you just created by typing `$newUser | fl *` and pressing **Enter**. The fl command is short for the command Format-List. Just as with the DSADD command, it would be impractical to use PowerShell in this manner to create user accounts. However, you can create PowerShell scripts that accept input from a user to automate the process of creating users. Creating complex PowerShell scripts is beyond the scope of this lab, but you should be aware of this scripting language.

15. Type **exit** and press **Enter** to exit PowerShell.

16. Stay logged on to Server1XX if you are going on to the next lab. Otherwise, log off Server1XX.

Review Questions

1. True or False? Windows PowerShell is a feature that is installed by default on Windows Server 2008.

2. The _____ uses syntax such as ou=myou,dc=mydomain,dc=com.

   a. UNC path

   b. distinguished name

   c. schema path

   d. common name

3. The _____ operator (|) is used to send the output of one command as input to another command.

   a. pipe

   b. forward

   c. logical or

   d. logical and

4. True or False? When a user account is created by PowerShell, the account is automatically made a member of the Guests group.

5. The _____ attribute on a user account is used to allow pre-Windows 2000 computers to log on to a domain.

Lab 5.2 Create User Templates and Change Schema Attribute Properties

Objectives
- Create a user template
- Modify the schema to change which attributes are copied from a user template

Materials Required
This lab requires the following:
- Server1XX

Estimated completion time: **20 minutes**

Activity Background
User templates are used to create user accounts that have similar properties, such as group memberships and other descriptive attributes. However, there are a number of attributes that are *not copied* when you copy a user template. This lab shows you where and how to modify schema attributes to change the results of the copy process.

Activity

1. If necessary, log on to Server1XX as Administrator, and open Active Directory Users and Computers.

2. Click to expand the domain node, if necessary. Click the **SalesMktg** OU. In the SalesMktg OU, create a global security group named **SalesMktg-G**. You'll add the user template to this group so that all users in the SalesMktg OU belong to this group by default.

3. In the SalesMktg OU, create a user with the full name **_SalesMktg Template** and the logon name **_SalesMktgTemplate**. Check the **Account is disabled** and **User must change password at next logon** check boxes, if necessary. There is no need to set the password on an account that is disabled, so you can leave the password fields blank.

4. Right-click the **_SalesMktg Template** user and click **Properties**.

5. If necessary, click the **General** tab. Type **Sales/Marketing User Account** in the Description text box, **Room 222** in the Office text box, **555-5555** in the Telephone number text box, and **books.tomsho.com** in the Web page text box.

6. Click the **Address** tab. Type **1022 First St.** in the Street text box, **Prescott** in the City text box, **AZ** in the State/province text box, and **12121** in the Zip/Postal Code text box. Click **United States** in the Country/region drop-down list.

7. Click the **Organization** tab. Type **Marketing Associate** in the Job Title text box, **Sales/Marketing** in the Department text box, and **Technical Treatises** in the Company text box.

8. Click the **Member Of** tab. Click **Add** to open the Select Groups dialog box. Type **SalesMktg-G** in the Enter the object names to select text box, click **Check Names**, and then click **OK** twice.

9. In the right pane of Active Directory Users and Computers, right-click the **_SalesMktg Template** user and click **Copy**. Type **Marketing** in the First name text box, **Associate1** in the Last name text box, and **mktgassoc1** in the User logon name text box, and then click **Next**.

10. Type **Password01** in the Password and Confirm password text boxes. Uncheck the **Account is disabled** check box, and then click **Next**. Click **Finish**.

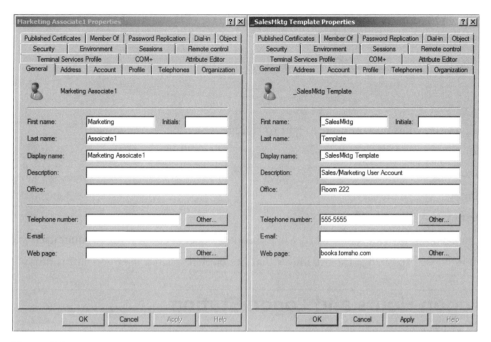

Figure 5-2   Comparing a template to a copy of the template

11. Right-click **Marketing Associate1** and click **Properties**. Arrange the Properties dialog box so that you can see the _SalesMktg Template user in Active Directory Users and Computers. Right-click **_SalesMktg Template** and click **Properties**. Arrange the two Properties dialog boxes side by side so that you can compare them (see Figure 5-2). Make sure the General tab is visible in both.

12. Notice that no fields in the template's General tab were copied to the Marketing Associate1 user. Click the **Address** tab in both Properties dialog boxes, and notice that the Street field wasn't copied. Click the **Organization** tab, and notice that the Job Title field wasn't copied.

13. Click the **Member Of** tab in both Properties dialog boxes, and notice that the group membership *was* copied.

14. Click **Cancel** to close both Properties dialog boxes, and leave Active Directory Users and Computers open.

15. A template user can be useful, but as you can see, many fields are not copied. It may be desirable to have some of these fields copied to make template users more useful. Fortunately, there is a way to specify additional fields to be copied. Open the **Schema Management** MMC you created in Lab 4.3, which you can find by clicking **Start**, **All Programs**, **Administrative Tools**.

16. Click to expand **Active Directory Schema**, if necessary. Click the **Attributes** folder.

17. In the middle pane scroll down until you find the streetAddress attribute. Double-click **streetAddress**. Check the **Attribute is copied when duplicating a user** check box and click **OK**. Do the same for the **title** and **WWHomePage** attributes. (You might think it would be a good idea to allow the password to be copied when duplicating a user; however, even though you can set the option for the password to be copied, the password is not copied.) Close Schema Management.

18. Copy the **_SalesMktg Template** account again, but this time, use the name **Marketing Associate2** with a logon name of **mktgassoc2**. In addition, be sure to uncheck the **Account is disabled** check box.

19. Double-click **Marketing Associate2** and verify that the Web page, Job Title, and Street Address fields have all been copied. Close all windows but stay logged on if you are going on to the next lab (click **No** when asked if you want to save the Schema Management console). If you are not going on to the next lab, shut down Server1XX.

Review Questions

1. True or False? The Department field is copied when you copy a user account.

2. Which of the following is copied when you copy a user account? (Choose all that apply.)

   a. City

   b. Company

   c. Web page

   d. Description

3. When duplicating a user, what do you need to edit to change which fields are copied?

   a. Schema classes

   b. Schema common names

   c. Schema attributes

   d. Schema properties

4. True or False? You need not provide a password when creating a user account if the account itself is disabled.

5. The _____ snap-in is used to change the attributes that are copied when a user account is duplicated.

Lab 5.3 Setting Logon Hours and Logon Station

Objectives

- Edit multiple Active Directory objects at once
- Set user logon hours to prevent users from logging on during certain days and hours
- Set user logon station to prevent users from logging on except at specified stations

Materials Required

- Server1XX and ServerCoreXX

Estimated completion time: **20 minutes**

Activity Background

Two of the properties of user accounts allow administrators to control when and from where a user can log onto the system, as follows:

- The Logon Hours property of a user account allows you to restrict the days and times that a user can log on to the domain. This attribute may be useful for maintaining and securing the network. For example, if most users should be logged on only from 7:00am to 10:00pm, Monday through Friday, you can restrict them from logging on late at night and weekends. Doing so also allows you to perform maintenance operations on the servers with the knowledge that users will not be logged on. It also prevents potential hackers from trying to log on to the system during off hours when the network is less monitored.

- The Log On To property of a user account allows you to restrict the stations from which a user can log on so you can ensure that user accounts with access to sensitive information can log on only from a limited number of computers. This precaution prevents, for example, a payroll department user from logging on from a station in another department where he or she might walk away from the station thereby giving whoever uses the station next access to payroll data.

This lab shows you how to edit multiple accounts simultaneously to change the default logon hours for those accounts. It then shows you how to edit an account to specify from which computer station the user can log on to the domain.

Activity

1. Start and log on to Server1XX as Administrator, if necessary, and then start ServerCoreXX. Log on to ServerCoreXX as **mktgassoc1** using **Password01**. When prompted to change your password, click **OK** and then change the password to **Password02**. Click **OK** to finish the logon.

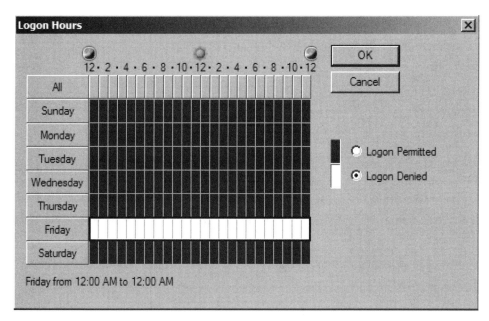

Figure 5-3 Deny logon hours for an entire day

2. Log on to Server1XX as **Administrator**, if necessary, and open Active Directory Users and Computers.

3. Click the **SalesMktg** OU. In the right pane, click **Marketing Associate1**, press **Ctrl** and click **Marketing Associate2** so that both users are selected. You can change properties of multiple users in this fashion.

4. Right-click one of the selected users and click **Properties**. In the Properties for Multiple Items dialog box, click the **Account** tab.

5. Check the **Logon hours** check box. Click the **Logon hours** button. Click and drag your mouse over the entire row of the current day. For example, if today is Friday, click and drag over the Friday row so that all columns are selected. Then click the **Logon Denied** option button. See Figure 5-3. Click **OK**, and then click **OK** again.

6. On ServerCoreXX, log off by typing **logoff** and pressing **Enter**.

7. Log on to ServerCoreXX as **mktgassoc1** again. You should get a message indicating that your account has time restrictions that prevent you from logging on. Click **OK**. Try logging on as **mktgassoc2**. You will be prompted to change your password. Change it to **Password02**. You should again see a message indicating that your account has a logon time restriction. Click **OK**. Your password change was not allowed and you are prompted to change it again. Click **Cancel**.

8. On Server1XX, repeat Steps 3 through 5, but on the Logon Hours screen, just click **OK** because you need not make any changes; that is, the hours are set to their default setting when multiple items are selected.

9. Log on to ServerCoreXX as **mktgassoc2**. You will be prompted to change the password. Change it to **Password02** and log on.

10. On Server1XX, double-click **Marketing Associate2**. Click the **Account** tab and click the **Log On To** button to open the Logon Workstations dialog.

11. Click the **The following computers** option button. In the Computer name box, type **Server1XX** and click **Add**. Click **OK**, and then click **OK**. Marketing Associate2 should be able to log on to Server1XX only.

12. On ServerCoreXX, type **logoff** and press **Enter** to log off Marketing Associate2. Try to log on to ServerCoreXX again using the mktgassoc2 account and Password02. You should see a message stating that your account is configured to prevent you from using this computer. Click **OK**.

13. On Server1XX, close all open windows and log off.

14. Log on as **mktgassoc2** to verify that you can do so. Log off Server1XX.

15. Shut down ServerCoreXX.

Review Questions

1. You can restrict user logon hours by which of the following criteria?

    a   Days of the week only

    b. Hours of the day only

    c. Hours, days, and months

    d. Days of the week and hours

2. To specify the station to which a user can log on, you must specify the _____.

    a. computer name

    b. distinguished name of the computer account

    c. MAC address of the computer

    d. domain\computer

3. Which of the following can be edited on multiple accounts at one time? (Choose all that apply.)

    a. Description

    b. Logon hours

    c. Password

    d. Display name

    e. Web page

4. True or False? By default, if a user is already logged on when the logon time restriction becomes effective, he or she is immediately logged off the system.

5. The command to log off a ServerCoreXX computer is _____.

Lab 5.4 Change Default Computer Location and Add a Client Computer Account to the Domain

Objectives

- Set a policy that restricts the creation of computer accounts
- Change the default location for new computer accounts
- Add a client computer account to the domain
- Manage a client computer from Active Directory

Materials Required

This lab requires the following:

- Server1XX and ClientXX

Estimated completion time: **20 minutes**

Activity Background

The default settings on a domain controller allow the members of the Authenticated Users group to add a workstation to the domain. Some administrators may wish to control the process more by restricting the 'Add workstations to domain' right to administrators or perhaps to a group that has IT personnel as its members. An administrator might also want to create the computer account first and then allow users to join the domain.

When a new computer account is created, by default it is placed in the Computers folder in Active Directory. Note, however, that because the Computers folder is not an OU, GPOs cannot be linked to it. To place computer accounts in an OU where a GPO can be linked, you can change the default location of newly created computer accounts using the **redircmp** command. You may wish to do this so that all new computer accounts are immediately subject to the policies you specify in GPOs linked to the new default location.

In this activity, you will restrict the computer account creation right to users in the IT-Group, which you will create in the InfoTech OU. Next, you will change the default location of newly created computer accounts. Finally, you will join your client computer to the domain.

Activity

1. Log on to Server1XX as Administrator, if necessary, and open Active Directory Users and Computers.

2. Click the **InfoTech** OU. Click the **Group** icon on the menu bar. In the Group name box, type **IT-Group**. Note that the Group scope is Global and the Group type is Security by default. Click **OK**.

3. Double-click **Mike NewTech** to open the Properties window. Click the **Member Of** tab. Notice that Mike NewTech is already a member of the Domain Users group. Click **Add**. Type **IT-Group** in the Enter the object names to select box and click **Check Names**. IT-Group is underlined, indicating that it is a valid group. Click **OK**, and then click **OK**.

4. Right-click the domain object (**W2k8AD1XX.local**) in Active Directory Users and Computers, point to **New** and click **Organizational Unit**. Type **MemberComputers** in the Name box and click **OK**. This will be the new default location for newly created computer accounts.

5. Open Group Policy Management. Click to expand the **Domain Controllers** OU and click **Default Domain Controllers Policy**. In the right pane, click the **Settings** tab. Click **show all**. You will see the Add workstations to domain policy under Local Policies/User Rights Assignment. That is the policy you are going to change.

6. Right-click **Default Domain Controllers Policy** and click **Edit** to start Group Policy Management Editor.

7. Under Computer Configuration, navigate to **Policies\Windows Settings\SecuritySettings\ Local Policies\User Rights Assignment**. In the right pane, double-click **Add workstations to domain**. Click **Authenticated Users** and click **Remove**.

8. Click **Add User or Group**. Type **IT-Group** in the User and group names box and click **OK**. Click **Add User or Group** again. Type **Administrators** and click **OK**. Click **OK**.

9. Close Group Policy Management Editor and Group Policy Management.

10. Open a command prompt. Type **redircmp ou=MemberComputers,dc=W2k8AD1XX,dc=local** and press **Enter**. You should see a message indicating the redirection was successful. Be sure that there are no spaces in the command except between redircmp and ou. If there are spaces in the distinguished name path, you must enclose the path in quotations. Close the command prompt.

11. Start your ClientXX computer and log on as **Administrator**.

12. Verify the IP address settings of your client computer. Its IP address must be in the 192.168.100.0 subnet and its Preferred DNS server must be 192.168.100.1XX (the address of Server1XX). Click **Start,** right-click **Network,** and click **Properties** to open the Network and Sharing Center.

13. In the Network and Sharing Center, click **Manage network connections**. Right-click **Local Area Connection** and click **Status**. Click the **Details** button. Verify that the settings are correct. Click **Close**. If any of the settings were not correct, click **Properties,** double-click **Internet Protocol Version 4,** and fix the settings as appropriate. (Note: If you see a User Account Control message here or in the future, click Continue.) Close all windows.

14. On ClientXX, click **Start,** right-click **Computer,** and click **Properties**. Click **Advanced system settings** to open the System Properties dialog.

15. Click the **Computer Name** tab. Click the **Change** button. Verify the computer name is ClientXX (or whatever your instructor specifies). If you need to change the computer name, do so now; restart the computer when prompted and return to the dialog box.

16. Click the **Domain** option button and type **W2k8AD1XX.local** in the text box. Click **OK**. You are prompted to enter a name and password. The name you enter here must be an account that has the right to create computer accounts in the domain.

17. Type **MNewTech** for the name and **Password01** for the password. Click **OK**. After a moment, you should get a message welcoming you to the domain. Click **OK**. A message is displayed informing you that you must restart your computer. Click **OK**. Click **Close**. Click **Restart Now** when prompted.

18. To verify that the computer account was created, open **Active Directory Users and Computers** on Server1XX if necessary. Click the **MemberComputers** OU. If you don't see the computer account, click the **Refresh** icon on the menu bar. You should see the ClientXX computer account in the MemberComputers OU. Remember, by default, new computer accounts are created in the Computers folder, but the redircmp command you used in Step 10 changed the default to the MemberComputers OU.

19. One advantage of computer accounts in Active Directory is the ability to remotely manage many aspects of the computer. Right-click the **ClientXX** computer account and click **Manage**. After a short delay, you should see a message indicating that the computer cannot be managed. This is due to firewall settings on the client computer. Click **OK**. Close the **Computer Management** MMC.

20. On ClientXX, log on as **domain administrator**. Click **Switch User**, click **Other User**, and type **W2k8AD1XX\administrator** in the User name box and **Password01** in the Password box and then click the arrow. (Note: The administrator account is the only account that requires you to preface the user name with the domain name. To log on to a member computer using another domain user, simply type the user name.)

21. On ClientXX, click **Start** and click **Control Panel**. In the Control Panel, click **Allow a program through Windows Firewall** under the Security category.

22. In the Windows Firewall Settings dialog, check the **Remote Administration** and **Remote Event Log Management** check boxes. Click **OK**.

23. Repeat Step 19 on Server1XX to manage ClientXX. Computer Management should successfully open. Notice the top node is labeled Computer Management (CLIENTXX.W2k8AD1XX.LOCAL) to indicate which computer is being managed (see Figure 5-4).

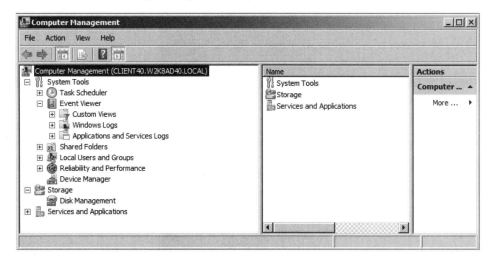

Figure 5-4 Remote management of a client computer

24. Close **Computer Management**. If you are going on to the next chapter immediately, close all open windows on Server1XX and ClientXX. Otherwise, shut down Server1XX and ClientXX.

Review Questions

1. Which of the following is the default location for new computer accounts?

   a. Domain Controllers OU

   b. Member Computers OU

   c. Computers Folder

   d. Users Folder

2. By default, members of which of the following groups has the right to add workstations to the domain?

   a. Everyone

   b. Authenticated Users

   c. Administrators

   d. Domain Users

3. When you right-click a computer account in Active Directory, which of the following options will you see?

   a. Connect to it using remote desktop protocol

   b. View its IP address settings

   c. Change the computer name

   d. Connect to it using Computer Management

4. True or False? The default location for new computer accounts can have a GPO linked to it.

5. The _____ command can change the default container for new computer objects to the NewClients OU in the mydomain.com domain.

5

CHAPTER SIX

WINDOWS FILE AND PRINT SERVICES

Labs included in this chapter

- Lab 6.1 Using File Encryption and EFS Certificates
- Lab 6.2 Create a Volume and Set Quotas Using File Server Resource Manager
- Lab 6.3 Creating a Share on Server Core and Setting Permissions on Folders Using ICACLS
- Lab 6.4 Install and Configure Distributed File System (DFS)

Microsoft MCTS Exam #70-640 Objectives

Objective

Windows File and Print Services are not a major part of the 70-640 objectives but are
included in this book because providing and securing access to file and printer resources
is tightly coupled with Active Directory user and group accounts.

Lab 6.1 Using File Encryption and EFS Certificates

Objectives
Encrypt a folder and its contents

- View certificates using the Certificates snap-in
- Backing up and restoring EFS certificates

Materials Required
This lab requires the following:

- Server1XX—Server1XX must be running when ClientXX is running
- ClientXX

Estimated completion time: **15 minutes**

Activity Background
The Encrypting File System (EFS) is a feature of NTFS whereby files can be encrypted on the hard drive, allowing only the user who encrypted the file access to its contents. Note that the certificate that is created when you first encrypt a file is necessary to decrypt the file. Thus, if the certificate file gets lost or damaged, you will be unable to access your encrypted file.

In this lab, you encrypt a file and then explore the Certificates snap-in, which allows you to view, delete, export, and import certificates. You will back up (export) your certificate and then delete the certificate file to simulate a lost or damaged certificate. Then you will verify that you cannot access your encrypted file. Finally, you will restore your certificate.

Activity

1. Start Server1XX. Start ClientXX and log on to the domain from ClientXX as **user1** with **Password02**.

2. Click **Start, Computer**. In the left pane of Windows Explorer, click the **Documents** folder under Favorite Links.

3. Create a text file in the Documents folder, and name it **Encrypted1**. Right-click **Encrypted1** and click **Properties**, and then click **Advanced** to open the Advanced Attributes dialog box for Encrypted1. Check the **Encrypt contents to secure data** check box, and then click **OK** twice. When you get the Encryption Warning message, click the **Encrypt the file only** option button, check the **Always encrypt only the file** check box, and then click **OK**.

4. Double-click **Encrypted1** to open it in Notepad, and type your name in it. Save the file, and exit Notepad.

5. Open the Advanced Attributes dialog box for Encrypted1, and click the **Details** button. Notice that user1 is listed as a user who can access the file, and Administrator is listed as a recovery agent. Click **Add**. Only user1's certificate is listed because no other user has been issued an EFS certificate on this computer. An EFS certificate is automatically issued when a user encrypts a file.

6. Click **View Certificate** to look at the contents of the EFS certificate. The certificate information lists the purposes for which the certificate can be used. Click **OK**, and then click **Cancel**. Click **OK** until all open properties dialog boxes are closed.

7. You can view and manage certificates using the Certificates snap-in. Click **Start,** type **MMC**, and then press **Enter**. Press **Ctrl+M** to open the Add or Remove Snap-ins dialog. Click **Certficates** and click **Add**. Click **OK**.

8. Click to expand the **Certficates** node. Click to expand **Personal** and click **Certificates**. In the middle pane, you will see the certificates issued to user1; in this case, there is only the EFS certificate. If necessary, scroll the middle pane to view the Expiration Date and Intended Purpose columns to verify that the certificate is an EFS certificate.

9a   e8   6b   b2

9. Double-click the **user1** certificate. Click the **Details** tab. Scroll down until you see the Thumbprint field. Write down the first four digits of the Thumbprint value—you will see this number again later. Click **OK**.

10. Right-click the **user1** certificate and point to **All Tasks**. You will see options to request a new certificate, renew the certificate, and export the certificate. It is a good idea to export your EFS certificate as a backup in case the certificate becomes damaged or lost. If that happens, you can import the backup so that you can access your encrypted files. Click **Export** to start the Certificate Export Wizard.

11. Click **Next**. In the Export Private Key window, click the **Yes, export the private key** option button and click **Next**. Click **Next** again.

12. In the Password screen, type **Password01** in both boxes, and then click **Next**.

13. In the File to Export window, click **Browse**. The default location for storing the exported certificate is in the Documents folder. Type **User1EFScert** in the File name box and click **Save**. Click **Next**. Click **Finish**. Click **OK** on the message indicating the export was successful. Open your Documents folder to verify the file is there.

14. In the MMC console, click **File** and click **Save As** to save the Certificates console. In the Save As dialog box, click **Desktop** and then type **Certs** in the File name box. Click **Save** to save the console to the desktop. Certificates are stored on the hard drive like any file. In Windows Server 2008 and Vista, they are stored in the user profile. In this case, the EFS certificate for user1 is stored in the path C:\Users\ user1\AppData\Roaming\Microsoft\SystemCertificates\My\Certificates. The AppData folder is hidden, so to access it, you must configure Windows Explorer to show hidden and system files. In the next part of this lab, you will access the certificate file.

15. From an Explorer window, click **Organize** and **Folder and Search Options**. Click the **View** tab. In the Advanced settings box, click the **Show hidden files and folders** option button and click **OK**. Navigate to the C:\Users\user1 folder. Double-click the **AppData** folder and then click **Roaming**, **Microsoft**, **SystemCertificates**, **My**, and **Certificates** folders. You will see a file whose name is the same as the number in the Thumbprint field you saw in Step 9.

16. To simulate a lost or corrupt certificate, click the file in the Certificates folder and press **Delete**. Click **Yes** to confirm.

17. The effect of the deleted certificate will not be apparent until you log off. To test this, log off and then log back on as **User1**.

18. Open your Documents folder where you saved the encrypted file earlier. Double-click **Encrypted1**. You should get an Access is denied message due to the fact that your EFS certificate has been deleted. Click **OK** and close Notepad.

19. At this point, you have two options to recover your encrypted files: you can use the Recovery Agent or you can restore your backed up certificate. Because you have a backup of the certificate, you'll use that method. Open the **Certs** console on your desktop that you saved earlier, and then navigate to the **Personal** folder to verify that the user1 EFS certificate is no longer there.

20. Right-click the **Personal** folder, point to **All Tasks**, and click **Import**. Click **Next**. Click **Browse**. In the left pane, click **Documents**. Click the **File name** list arrow, and click **Personal Information Exchange**. You should see the User1EFScert that you exported earlier.

21. Click **User1EFScert** and click **Open**. Click **Next**. Type **Password01** in the Password box. Check the **Mark this key as exportable** check box so that you can back up the key again if necessary. Click **Next**, click **Next** again, click **Finish**, and then click **OK**.

22. Double-click the **Certificates** folder under Personal to verify the certificate is there. Close the Certs console. Click **No** when prompted to save changes.

23. Open your Documents folder and verify that you can again open the Encrypted1 file. Close **Notepad**.

24. Shut down ClientXX. Stay logged on Server1XX if you are going on to the next lab. Otherwise, shut down Server1XX.

Review Questions

1. True or False? An EFS certificate is automatically issued when a user encrypts a file.

2. EFS certificates are stored in the_____.

   a. users Documents folder

   b. Windows\System\Certificates folder

   c. Certificates database

   d. AppData folder in the user's profile

3. Which of the following should you do to access an encrypted file after the related certificate has been damaged or deleted? (Choose all that apply.)

   a. Restore the certificate

   b. Uncheck the encryption attribute

   c. Use the Recovery Agent

   d. Take ownership of the encrypted file

4. True or False? Any user can be added to the list of users who may access an encrypted file.

5. The _____ is a Recovery Agent in a default Windows domain environment.

Lab 6.2 Create a Volume and Set Quotas Using File Server Resource Manager

Objectives

- Install file server resource manager (FSRM)
- Create a new disk volume
- Enable disk quotas using FSRM

Materials Required

This lab requires the following:

- Server1XX
- A second disk on Server1XX

Estimated completion time: **20 minutes**

Activity Background

File Server Resource Manager (FSRM) is new in Windows Server 2008. FSRM allows an administrator to assign quotas to volumes and folders and to restrict the types of files that users can store on volumes. In addition, FSRM lets you create quota templates that can be applied to volumes so that quotas can be configured uniformly across your volumes.

Share and Storage Management is an MMC that lets you provision storage by creating volumes and shares. In this activity, you create a new volume using Share and Storage Management and assign quotas to that volume using FSRM.

Activity

1. Log on to Server1XX as Administrator, if necessary.

2. Start Server Manager, if necessary.

3. Click the **Roles** node in Server Manager and in the right pane click **File Services** under Roles Summary.

4. Scroll down until you see Role Services. You should see that one role service is installed. Click **Add Role Services**.

5. On the Select Role Services screen, click **File Server Resource Manager** and click **Next**.

6. On the Configure Storage Usage Monitoring screen, click **Next**. Click **Install**. After the installation completes, click **Close**. Close **Server Manager**.

7. Before you use FSRM, you need to create a new volume. Click **Start**, point to **Administrative Tools**, and click **Share and Storage Management**.

8. In the right pane, click **Provision Storage** to start the Provision Storage Wizard. In the Storage Source screen, click the **On one or more disks available on this server** option button, if necessary, and click **Next**.

9. On the Disk Drive screen, click **Disk 1** if necessary and click **Next**.

10. On the Volume Size screen, specify a size of **1 GB**. Click **Next**.

11. On the Volume Creation screen, click the drive letter drop-down arrow and select the **G** drive. Click **Next**.

12. On the Format screen, you will notice that no option is given to select a file format. NTFS is always selected when you provision storage using Share and Storage Management. In addition, NTFS is the required format when you wish to use disk quotas. Type **Data1** in the Volume label text box and click **Next**. Click **Create**. On the Confirmation screen, once the volume is created, click **Close**.

13. Close Share and Storage Management.

14. Click **Start**, point to **Administrative Tools**, and click **File Server Resource Manager**.

15. Expand **Quota Management**, if necessary, and click **Quotas**.

16. In the right pane, click **Create Quota**. On the Create Quota screen, click **Browse**. Click the **Data1 (G:)** volume. Note that you can select a folder, so quotas need not apply to an entire volume. Click **OK**.

17. Review the rest of the Create Quota screen. The default quota limit is 100MB. You can choose from several other pre-defined quota properties or define custom quota properties. Accept the defaults and click **Create**.

18. Click **Start** and click **Computer** to open Explorer.

19. Notice the Data1 volume. The size you created was 1.0 GB, but it only shows as 100 MB in the Total Size column, reflecting the quota value you assigned to it. Unlike when you create quotas from the Quotas tab of the volume's properties, quotas created using FSRM apply to the administrator as well as regular users. Close Explorer.

20. Return to FSRM and in the middle pane, right-click the quota you created and click **Delete Quotas**. Click **Yes**.

21. Close all open windows. Stay logged on Server1XX if you are going on to the next lab. Otherwise, shut down Server1XX.

Review Questions

1. Which of the following is not a role service available with the File Services role?

   a. Distribute File System

   b. File Server Resource Manager

   c. File Transfer Protocol Services

   d. Services for Network File System

2. What is true about the volume on which you configure quotas?

   a. It must be formatted as NTFS.

   b. Quotas must be configured for the entire volume.

   c. The volume can be formatted FAT32 or NTFS, but not FAT16.

   d. The volume must be at least 10GB in size.

3. True or False? FSRM is the only method available for creating quotas in Windows Server 2008.

4. True or False? FSRM is installed by default when the File Services role is installed.

5. In Windows Server 2008, you can use Disk Management or _____ to create a new volume.

Lab 6.3 Creating a Share on Server Core and Setting Permissions on Folders Using ICACLS

Objectives

- Create a share using the command-line on Server Core
- Set permissions using ICACLS

Materials Required

This lab requires the following:

- Server1XX
- ServerCoreXX

Estimated completion time: **20 minutes**

Activity Background

Server Core can be managed remotely using MMCs, but you might need to perform some tasks quickly on a Server Core computer while you are logged onto the console. To perform such tasks, you can use the net share command to share a folder and the icacls command to change the NTFS permissions on folders and files.

The icacls command has many options and this lab explores only the basics. For more information on using icacls, visit http://technet.microsoft.com/en-us/library/cc753525%28WS.10%29.aspx.

Activity

1. Make sure Server1XX is started. Log on to ServerCoreXX as the domain Administrator.

2. First, view existing shares on ServerCoreXX by typing **net share** and pressing **Enter** from the command prompt. You should see the default administrative shares listed: C$, IPC$, and ADMIN$.

3. To create a new folder on the root of the C: drive named CoreShare, type **mkdir \CoreShare** and press **Enter**.

4. Next, type **net share CoreShare=c:\CoreShare** and press **Enter**. In that command, CoreShare is the name of the share as it will be seen on the network and C:\CoreShare is the path to the folder to be shared.

5. Type **net share coreshare** and **press Enter** to view the properties of the new share. Notice that the permission is set to Everyone Read by default. You might want something different than that, but note that once the share is created, you cannot change the permission using net share. To effect a change, you must first delete the share and recreate it by specifying the permissions you want.

6. Type **net share CoreShare /delete** and press **Enter**. The share is deleted (but the folder is not). Type **net share CoreShare=c:\CoreShare /Grant:Everyone,Full** and press **Enter**. Type **net share CoreShare** and press **Enter** to display the settings. You can include multiple /Grant: parameters to include multiple users or groups in the permissions list.

7. To set the NTFS permissions on the C:\Coreshare folder, you use the icacls command. Type **icacls c:\CoreShare** and press **Enter**. The current permissions are listed. The letters such as OI, CI, and IO in parentheses indicate the inheritance property of the permission. The letters you see such as F and R indicate the permission (F=Full Control, R=Read).

8. To change the permissions so that Users have Modify permissions, type **icacls c:\CoreShare /grant Users:(OI)(CI)M** and press **Enter**. Be sure that there are no spaces after Modify:.

9. Verify that you can access the share from another computer. Log on to Server1XX as **Administrator** if necessary. Click **Start**. In the Start Search box, type **\\ServerCoreXX\CoreShare** and press **Enter**. An Explorer window should open.

10. Right-click in the right pane of the Explorer window, point to **New**, and click **Text Document** to verify that you can create files in the share.

11. Right-click the **CoreShare** folder in Explorer and click **Properties**. Click the **Security** tab. Click the **Users** entry in the top pane. The bottom pane should show that Users have the Modify permission.

12. Close all open windows on Server1XX. Stay logged on to both servers if you are going on to the next lab immediately; otherwise shutdown both servers.

Review Questions

1. True or False? There are three shares by default on a Windows member server.

2. Which of the following is true about the net share command?

   a. By default, Everyone is given Full Control.

   b. You must specify permissions when creating a share.

   c. By default, Everyone has the Read permission.

   d. Only a single user or group can be given permissions.

3. Which of the following is an administrative share on a member server? (Choose all that apply.)

   a. Sysvol$

   b. ADMIN$

   c. IPC$

   d. System$

4. True or False? You must delete a share if you want to change its permission settings using net share.

5. The _____ command shares the c:\mktdocs folder using the share name Marketing.

Lab 6.4 Install and Configure Distributed File System (DFS)

Objectives

- Install DFS
- Configure a DFS root and add shares

Materials Required

This lab requires the following:

- Server1XX
- ServerCoreXX

Estimated completion time: **20 minutes**

Activity Background

The more servers you have in a domain, the more likely your shares are to be spread among many servers. This arrangement can be confusing and frustrating for users because they need to know the UNC path to all of these shares or search for them if the shares are published in Active Directory.

DFS provides a tool for an administrator to consolidate many shares in a single location from the user's standpoint. Users need only know the name of the domain and the name of the DFS namespace to access several shares that might be hosted on several servers. For example, to access all the shares in the DFS namespace named coolshares in the domain coolgadgets.local, the user need only know \\coolgadgets.local\coolshares. He or she does need to know that several shares are listed as folders under the namespace, or root, of DFS.

In this lab, you install the DFS role service and then configure it to host the two shares you have created during the course of these labs: PublishedShare, which is on Server1XX, and CoreShare, which is on ServerCoreXX.

Activity

1. Log on to Server1XX as Administrator, if necessary, and open Server Manager.

2. Expand the **Roles** node and click **File Services**. In the right pane, scroll down to Role Services.

3. Click **Add Role Services**. On the Select Role Services screen, click **Distribute File System**. Click **Next**.

4. On the Create a DFS Namespace screen, type **W2k8Shares** and click **Next**. W2k8Shares will be the root of your DFS namespace.

5. On the Select Namespace Type screen, click **Next**. On the Configure Namespace screen, click **Next**. You will configure the namespace further using the DFS Management MMC. Click **Install**.

6. After the installation is complete, click **Close**.

7. Click **Start**, point to **Administrative Tools,** and click **DFS Management**.

8. Click to expand **Namespaces** in the left pane. Click the **\\W2k8AD1XX.local\W2k8Shares** namespace.

9. In the right pane, click **New Folder**. In the New Folder window, type **Share1** in the Name text box. Click **Add**.

10. Next to the Path to folder target box, click **Browse**. Click **PublishedShare**, if necessary, and click **OK**. You created PublishedShare in Chapter 3. Click **OK** again. Note that for redundancy, you can have multiple Folder targets for each DFS share. For example, you could have a share on two different servers, and DFS will replicate the data between them to keep them synchronized. The servers will load balance, and if one server goes down, the data will still be available. Click **OK** again.

11. In DFS Management, click **New Folder** again. Type **Share2** in the Name text box. Click **Add**. Next to the Path to folder target box, click **Browse**. Click **Browse** next to the Server box.

12. In the Select Computer dialog, type **ServerCoreXX** and click **Check Names**. Click **OK**.

13. Click **CoreShare** if necessary in the Shared folders box and click **OK**. CoreShare is the share you created earlier in Lab 6.3. Click **OK** until you are back to DFS Management.

14. In DFS Management, click to expand **\\W2k8AD1XX.local\W2k8Shares**. Your DFS Management screen should look like Figure 6-1.

15. To see DFS in action, click **Start**, type **\\W2k8AD1XX\w2k8shares** in the Start Search box, and press **Enter**.

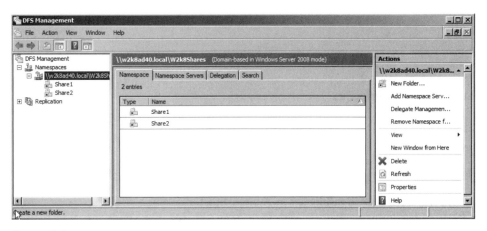

Figure 6-1   DFS Management

16. An Explorer window will open showing you the Share1 and Share2. Double-click **Share2** and verify that it contains the text document you created in Lab 6-3. As you can see, DFS allows you to simplify the access to shared folders throughout your domain. Rather than users having to know which servers hosted which shares, you need only access the root of the DFS namespace, in this case \\W2k8AD1XX.local\W2k8Shares. You can even map a drive to W2k8Shares to have all the shares just a drive letter away.

17. Close all open windows. If you are going on to the next chapter, remain logged on to Server1XX; otherwise, log off Server1XX. Shut down ServerCoreXX.

Review Questions

1. True or False? The name under the domain name in a DFS namespace is referred to as the DFS root.

2. Which of the following are reasons to associate more than one share with a single DFS folder? (Choose all that apply.)

   a. To have multiple sets of permissions

   b. To access the DFS folder with more than one name

   c. For fault tolerance in case a server hosting a share goes down

   d. For load balancing

3. Which of the following role services allows you to consolidate multiple shares in a single location?

   a. File Server Resource Manager

   b. Windows Search Service

   c. File Replication Service

   d. Distributed File System

4. True or False? You cannot map a drive letter to a DFS namespace.

5. The _____ command accesses a DFS folder named MyDocs in a DFS namespace called MyShares in the domain mydomain.com.

CONFIGURING GROUP POLICY

Labs included in this chapter

- Lab 7.1 Configuring and Testing Group Policy Loopback Processing
- Lab 7.2 GPO Inheritance Blocking, Enforcement, and Results
- Lab 7.3 Configure a Software Deployment GPO
- Lab 7.4 Configuring WMI Filtering and Group Policy Modeling

Microsoft MCTS Exam #70-640 Objectives

Objective	Lab
Create and apply Group Policy Objects	7.1

Lab 7.1 Configuring and Testing Group Policy Loopback Processing

Objectives

- Create a Group Policy Object (GPO) and set user policies
- Test a GPO's affect on users
- Configure and test GPO loopback processing

Materials Required

This lab requires the following:

- Server1XX—Server1XX must be running when ClientXX is running
- ClientXX

Estimated completion time: **20 minutes**

Activity Background

Companies commonly place computers in corporate lobbies, conference rooms, and other public areas to facilitate access to corporate resources by visitors. In such situations, administrators might prefer a common desktop appearance, regardless of who logs on. GPO loopback processing allows an administrator to place all common area computers into a single OU and apply a user configuration policy that affects all users who log on to the computers.

Activity

1. Start and log on to Server1XX as Administrator.

2. Click **Start**, point to **Administrative Tools**, and click **Group Policy Management** to open the Group Policy Management Console (GPMC).

3. Click the **Group Policy Objects** folder. In the right pane, right-click in empty space and click **New**.

4. In the New GPO dialog, type **LBtestGPO** and click **OK**.

5. Right-click **LBtestGPO** and click **Edit** to start the Group Policy Management Editor (GPME).

6. Under the User Configuration node, click to expand **Policies** and then **Administrative Templates**. Click **Start Menu and Taskbar**.

7. In the right pane, double-click **Remove Music icon from Start Menu**. Click the **Enabled** option button. Click **OK**.

8. In the right pane, double-click **Add the Run command to the Start Menu**. Click the **Enabled** option button, click **OK**, and then close the GPME.

9. In GPMC, right-click the **Development** OU and click **Link an Existing GPO**. In the Select GPO dialog, click **LBtestGPO** and click **OK**.

10. Expand the **Development** OU and click **LBtestGPO**. In the right pane, click the **Settings** tab and click **show all**. You should see the Start Menu and Taskbar settings you configured.

11. From your ClientXX computer, log on to the domain as **DevUser1** with **Password02**. You are prompted to change your password. Click **OK**. Type **Password03** twice and click the arrow. Click **OK** again.

12. Once logged on, click **Start** and verify that the Music folder is not shown and that the Run command has been added to the Start menu. Log off ClientXX.

13. On Server1XX, open **GPMC** if necessary. Unlink LBtestGPO from the Development OU by right-clicking **LBtestGPO** and clicking **Delete**. Click **OK**.

14. Next, you need to link LBtestGPO to the MemberComputers OU where your ClientXX computer account is located. To do so, right-click the **MemberComputers** OU and click **Link an Existing GPO**. In the Select GPO dialog box, click **LBtestGPO** and click **OK**.

15. Log on to the domain from ClientXX as **DevUser1**. Verify that the Start menu no longer has the Run command and again has the Music folder. Because you unlinked LBtestGPO from the Development OU where DevUser1 is located, DevUser1 no longer is in the scope of LBtestGPO. (If the Run command is still on the Start menu, run gpupdate from a command prompt.)

16. On Server1XX, click to expand the **MemberComputers** OU and right-click **LBtestGPO** and click **Edit**. You will set this policy to enable loopback group policy processing.

17. Expand **Computer Configuration**, **Policies**, **Administrative Templates**, **System**, and then click the **Group Policy** folder.

18. In the right pane, scroll down to find the **User Group Policy loopback processing mode** policy and double-click it. Click the **Enabled** option button. Leave the Mode setting as Replace. Click the **Explain** tab to read more about this policy. Click **OK**, and then close GPME.

19. On ClientXX, click **Start**, type **gpupdate** in the Start Search box, and press **Enter**. When gpupdate completes, log off and log on again as **DevUser1**.

20. You should see that the Run command is on the Start menu and that the Music folder is no longer there. The loopback processing policy causes the policies in the User Configuration section to be applied to all users who log on to the computers in the MemberComputers OU even though their accounts are not in the scope of the GPO. Log off ClientXX.

21. On Server1XX, unlink LBtestGPO from the MemberComputers OU by right-clicking **LBtestGPO** and clicking **Delete** and then clicking **OK**. Log off both Server1XX and ClientXX if you are going on to the next lab; otherwise, shut down both computers.

Review Questions

1. True or False? Policies set in the User Configuration section of a GPO normally affect user accounts only in the scope of the GPO.

2. Which of the following best describes group policy loopback processing?

   a. Policies in the Computer Configuration section are applied to all users whose accounts are in the scope of the GPO.

   b. Policies in the User Configuration section are applied to all users who log on to a computer that is in the scope of the GPO.

   c. Policies in the Computer Configuration section are applied to any computer onto which a user logs—if the user account is in the scope of the GPO.

   d. The GPO inherits policies only from the User Configuration of GPOs that is linked to parent containers.

3. Which of the following is the correct path to the loopback processing policy?

   a. Computer Configuration\Policies\Administrative Templates\System\Group Policy

   b. Computer Configuration\Policies\Administrative Templates\Windows Components\Group Policy

   c. User Configuration\Policies\Windows Settings\System\Group Policy

   d. User Configuration\Policies\Administrative Templates\System\Group Policy

4. True or False? Group policy loopback processing can ensure a common desktop look for each user who logs on to a computer affected by the processing.

5. _____ is a command that will cause group policies to be downloaded to a computer immediately.

Lab 7.2 GPO Inheritance Blocking, Enforcement, and Results

Objectives

- Block GPO Inheritance
- Enforce GPO Processing
- Run Group Policy Results

Materials Required

This lab requires the following:

- Server1XX
- ClientXX

Estimated completion time: **20 minutes**

Activity Background

The normal processing of GPOs causes all computers and users in the scope of a GPO to be affected by that GPO's settings. GPOs are processed in this order: Local policies, Site policies, Domain policies, and OU policies. If any conflicts exist, the last policy to be applied takes precedence.

Normal GPO processing can be altered by using GPO Inheritance Blocking, Enforcement, and filtering. This lab explores the use of GPO Inheritance Blocking and Enforcement. It then uses the Group Policy Results tool to examine a report that describes how GPOs were processed for a particular set of objects. In Lab 7.4, you will use WMI filtering to examine how filtering can affect GPO processing.

Activity

1. Log on to Server1XX as Administrator, if necessary.

2. Open Active Directory Users and Computers. Click the **Development** OU. Create a new OU in Development named **Hardware**. Then, create a user in the Hardware OU named **HwUser1** with **Password01**. Make sure HwUser1 does *not* have to change the password when he or she logs on.

3. Open GPMC, and click the **Group Policy Objects** folder. Create a GPO in this folder named **DevGPO**. (Refer to Lab 7-1, if you need a reminder of how to create a GPO.)

4. In the right pane, right-click **DevGPO** and click **Edit**. In GPME, expand **User Configuration**, **Policies**, **Administrative Templates** and then click **Control Panel**.

5. Set the Force classic Control Panel view to **Enable** and then click **OK**.

6. Close GPME. In GPMC, link the DevGPO GPO to the Development OU. (Refer to Lab 7.1 for a reminder of how to link GPOs to containers.)

7. Expand the **Development** OU, if necessary, and then click the **Hardware** OU. In the right pane, click the **Group Policy Inheritance** tab. Notice that Hardware is inheriting policies from both DevGPO and Default Domain Policy and DevGPO has a stronger precedence than Default Domain Policy. Remember, GPOs linked to the same object are applied in reverse order of their Precedence number, which means DevGPO in this case is applied last, giving it precedence. Leave GPMC open.

8. If you haven't restarted ClientXX since the last lab, do so now. Log on to the domain from ClientXX as **HwUser1** with **Password01**.

9. Click **Start** and click **Control Panel**. The Control Panel should be in classic view mode (if it is not, run gpupdate and log off and back on again). Notice that you cannot change the view mode back to category view mode. You cannot change the mode because it is configured by Group Policy. Close Control Panel.

10. On Server1XX, in the left pane of GPMC, right-click the **Hardware** OU under the Development OU and click **Block Inheritance**. Notice that the list of GPOs in the Group Policy Inheritance tab is now empty.

11. On ClientXX, open a command prompt window. Type **gpupdate** and press **Enter**. After Gpupdate.exe updates group policies, close the command prompt window. (You can also log off and back on again to update user policies.)

12. Click **Start** and click **Control Panel**. The Control Panel is still in Classic View but you can change it back to category view mode by clicking **Control Panel Home**. The fact that you can change the view mode indicates that the group policy is no longer in affect. Close Control Panel.

13. You can override the Block Inheritance option by enforcing the GPO. On Server1XX in GPMC, right-click the **DevGPO** linked to the Development OU and click **Enforced**. Click the **Hardware** OU and click the **Group Policy Inheritance** tab in the right pane, if necessary. If the DevGPO is not listed, click the **Refresh** icon on GPMC. As you can see, an enforced GPO overrides the Block Inheritance option.

14. One way to check how group policies are being applied to a user and/or a computer is to use the Group Policy Results tool. In GPMC, right-click the **Group Policy Results** folder and click **Group Policy Results Wizard**. Click **Next**.

15. On the Computer Selection screen, click the **Another computer** option button. Type **ClientXX**. Note that you can omit computer settings if you wish by clicking the Do not display policy settings for the selected computer in the results check box. Click **Next**.

16. On the User Selection screen, click **W2k8AD1XX\HwUser1** and click **Next**. You can also choose to exclude user settings from the results if desired.

17. Click **Next**. Once completed, click **Finish**.

18. On the Group Policy Results Summary tab, click **show all**.

19. In the Computer Configuration Summary, you will see that the Default Domain Policy is the only policy being applied. Scroll down to the User Configuration Summary. Note that under Applied GPOs, you will see None. You might find this odd due to the fact that DevGPO should be affecting HwUser1. However, Group Policy Results shows only what policies have already been applied to a user or computer. Because you have not logged on since you set DevGPO to Enforced, the results don't reflect it.

20. On your ClientXX computer, run gpudpate.

21. After gpupdate completes, go back to Server1XX and under the Group Policy Results folder, right-click the **HwUser1 on ClientXX** report and click **Rerun Query**.

22. View the User Configuration Summary again. You should see that DevGPO is now being applied. Click the **Settings** tab and click **show all**. You will see all the settings being applied to the computer account and further down on the screen, you will see the Force classic Control Panel view policy.

23. Close all open windows on Server1XX and ClientXX. Log off both Server1XX and ClientXX if you are going on to the next lab; otherwise, shut down both computers.

Review Questions

1. Which of the following is true about group policy inheritance?

   a. It cannot be blocked.

   b. By default, GPOs linked to a parent object take precedence over GPOs linked to child objects.

   c. When multiple GPOs are linked to the same object, the GPO with the lower number link order takes precedence.

   d. If a GPO is enforced, it still won't affect an OU that has Block Inheritance selected.

2. When you configure the Computer Configuration of a GPO, _____ will make the GPO take effect on the computers in its scope. (Choose all that apply.)

   a. logging off a computer and logging back on to a computer in the GPO's scope

   b. running gpupdate on a computer in the GPO's scope

   c. restarting a computer in the GPO's scope

   d. running gpupdate on the domain controller on which the policy was configured

3. True or False? Group policy Enforcement is set on GPOs and Block Inheritance is set on OUs.

4. True or False? Group Policy Results shows a report of what will happen to a user or computer the next time the current policy configuration is applied.

5. If you want to ensure that a GPO's policies are applied to objects in child containers, you should enable the _____ option on the GPO.

Lab 7.3 Configure a Software Deployment GPO

Objectives

- Configure a software deployment GPO

Materials Required

This lab requires the following:

- Server1XX
- ClientXX

Estimated completion time: **20 minutes**

Activity Background

Maintaining software is one of the most difficult and time consuming tasks for an IT administrator. Fortunately, the Software Installation policy can ease some of the angst that maintaining software can cause. For instance, you can automatically install software for a group of computers or users in an OU, or you can make software available for users to install if desired. Furthermore, you can automatically uninstall software if the user or computer falls outside the scope of the policy or if the package is removed from the policy. In addition, software can also be automatically updated.

In this lab, you deploy a software package using the assign option for users so that the package is installed when the user logs on.

Activity

1. Log on to Server1XX as Administrator, if necessary.

2. Open Windows Explorer, and navigate to the **Data1** volume. Create a new folder called **SwDeploy** in this volume.

3. Right-click **SwDeploy** and click **Share**. In the File Sharing Wizard, type **Authenticated Users** in the text box at the top, and then click **Add**. The default permission of Reader is sufficient. Leave Administrator in the permissions list at the bottom. Click **Share**, and then click **Done**.

4. In Windows Explorer, expand the **SwDeploy** folder, and create a subfolder named **XMLNotePad**. (XML NotePad is the name of the utility you're deploying.) Close all open windows on your server.

5. Start Internet Explorer and go to **www.microsoft.com/download**. In the Search text box, type **xmlnotepad** and click the magnifying glass icon. (If you click Web, you will get more results but the first link should get you to the download site.)

6. Click **XML Notepad 2007**. Click the **Download** button on the XML Notepad 2007 page. Click **Save**.

7. In the Save As dialog, click **Browse Folders** and click **Computer** under Favorite Links. Double-click the **Data1** volume, double-click **SwDeploy**, double-click **XMLNotePad**, and click **Save**. Once the download is complete, click **Close**.

8. On Server1XX, open GPMC. Click to expand **Domains** and **W2k8AD1XX.local**, if necessary. Click the **Group Policy Objects** folder, and create a GPO in it named **SwDeployUser**. Right-click **SwDeployUser** and click **Edit**. In the GPME, click to expand **User Configuration**, **Policies**, **Software Settings**, and click **Software Installation**.

9. Right-click the **Software Installation** extension, point to **New**, and click **Package**. In the Open dialog box, type **\\Server1XX\SwDeploy\XMLNotePad** and click **Open**. Click the **XmlNotepad.msi** file, and then click **Open**.

10. In the Deploy Software dialog box, click the **Advanced** option button and click **OK**. Click the **Deployment** tab. Review the possible options for the deployment of software to users. Under Deployment type, click **Assigned**. Note that the option to Auto-install this application by file extension activation becomes grayed out. Check the **Install this application at logon** check box. Browse the rest of the tabs to review possible deployment options. Click **OK**.

11. Close GPME. In GPMC, link the **SwDeployUser** GPO to the **Development** OU.

12. If necessary, log off ClientXX and then log back on as **DevUser1**. Sometimes, it takes two logons before the application will install. If you don't see a shortcut to XML Notepad 2007 on your desktop, log off and log on again as **DevUser1**.

13. XML Notepad can be a handy editor to work with XML files and Group Policy definition files that have an ADMX extension. Close all open windows on ClientXX and Server1XX. Log off both Server1XX and ClientXX if you are going on to the next lab; otherwise, shut down both computers.

Review Questions

1. True or False? There is a Software Installation node in both the Computer Configuration and User Configuration sections of a GPO.

2. Which of the following is true about software installation options?

    a. You can deploy software setup files that have a zip, exe, or msi extension.

    b. Software deployment to a computer can only be assigned, not published.

    c. Software deployment to a user can only be assigned, not published.

    d. There must be a mapped drive to the shared folder that holds the software setup file.

3. Which of the following is true about software installation? (Choose all that apply.)

    a. Assigning the package to a computer installs the software automatically.

    b. Publishing the package to a user installs the software automatically.

    c. Assigning the package to a user installs the software at next logon by default.

    d. Publishing the package to a user makes the software available to the user for installation.

4. True or False? Once software is installed via Group Policy, it can only be uninstalled manually.

5. You should choose the _____ deployment type when you want to have the option for the software to install automatically the next time the user logs on.

Lab 7.4 Configuring WMI Filtering and Group Policy Modeling

Objectives

- Configure WMI Filtering
- Configure Group Policy Results
- Configure Group Policy Modeling

Materials Required

This lab requires the following:

- Server1XX
- ClientXX
- ServerCoreXX

Estimated completion time: **20 minutes**

Activity Background

You might need to apply group policies based not on where a computer account is located, but on properties of the actual computers in the domain. To do so, you can create filters based on group memberships. This type of filtering is called security filtering. Note, however, that there might be problems with filtering based solely on group memberships. For instance, what if you had an application to install via Group Policy that could be installed only on Vista or Windows 7 computers and not on XP computers? In addition, what if you had member computers that had Server 2008 installed and you wanted to restrict user logons but the respective computer accounts were in the same OUs as Vista, XP, and Windows 7 computers? Fortunately, WMI filters allow you to filter to which computers a GPO will apply based on properties of the computer. Some of the properties that you can specify include operating system, disk drive properties, free memory, CPU features, time zone, network adapter properties, service pack installed, computer manufacturer, and others.

You can learn more about WMI filtering from these two TechNet sites:

- http://technet.microsoft.com/en-us/library/cc779036%28WS.10%29.aspx

- http://blogs.technet.com/johnbaker/archive/2006/02/22/420286.aspx

Activity

1. Log on to Server1XX as Administrator, if necessary, and open Active Directory Users and Computers.

2. Move ClientXX from the MemberComputers OU to the MemberServers OU. Both ServerCoreXX and ClientXX are now in the MemberServers OU.

3. Open Group Policy Management.

4. Click the **WMI Filters** folder, right-click in the right pane, and click **New**. Type **Server2008** in the Name box and in the Description box, type **All computers running Windows Server 2008**.

5. Click **Add**. Type **Select * from Win32_OperatingSystem where (caption like "%2008%")** and click **OK**. That WMIC command will select only those computers whose operating system name contains the string "2008". Your WMIC query should look like Figure 7-1. You can add additional conditions to the query. For example, you could specify conditions based upon available disk space, network settings, and even computer manufacturer. Click **Save**.

6. In GPMC, expand the **Group Policy Objects** folder and click **MemberServers-Logon**.

7. Click the **Scope** tab, if necessary, and in the WMI Filtering section, click the drop-down arrow and click **Server2008**. Click **Yes**. Verify that this GPO is still linked to the MemberServers OU by looking in the Links section of the Scope tab. If the GPO is not linked, link it now.

8. Start your ClientXX computer (if it was already turned on, restart it to be sure all computer policies are applied). Remember, the MemberServers-Logon GPO restricts local logon only to Server Operators and Administrators.

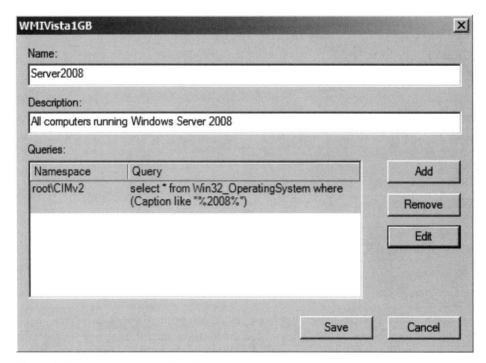

Figure 7-1   Creating a WMIC filter for Group Policy processing

9. When ClientXX reboots, try to log on as **DevUser1** with **Password03**. You should still be able to do so because the WMI filter restricts the application of the MemberServers-Logon GPO to computers that are running Windows Server 2008. Your ClientXX computer, which is running a different OS, is therefore excluded from that GPO.

10. Start ServerCoreXX and try to log on as **DevUser1**. You will get an error message stating that the logon method is not allowed.

11. On Server1XX, right-click **Group Policy Results** and click **Group Policy Results Wizard**. Click **Next**.

12. On the Computer Selection screen, click the **Another computer** option button and click **Browse**. Type **ClientXX** and click **Check Names**. Click **OK**, and then click **Next**.

13. Click the **Do not display user policy settings** option button and click **Next**. Click **Next**, and then click **Finish**.

14. In the right pane, on the Summary tab, click **show all**. Under the Group Policy Objects section, notice that the Default Domain Policy is listed under Applied GPOs and that MemberServers-Logon is listed under Denied GPOs because of the False WMI Filter. Review the WMI Filters section a little further down and you will see that the Server2008 WMI Filter has the value False.

7

15. Repeat Steps 11 through 14, except this time type **ServerCoreXX** instead of ClientXX in Step 12. You should see that the MemberServers-Logon GPO was applied and that the WMI Filter has a value of True.

16. Remember, the Group Policy Results wizard shows the actual results of how group policies have been applied to a computer or user. Group Policy Modeling is more of a 'what if' program that shows what the results of a GPO configuration might be given certain circumstances. Click the **Group Policy Modeling** folder.

17. In the right pane in Group Policy Modeling, right-click and click **Group Policy Modeling Wizard**. Click **Next**.

18. On the Domain Controller Selection window, click the **This domain controller** option button and click **Next**.

19. On the User and Computer Selection screen, in the Computer information section, click the **Computer** option button and click **Browse**. In the Select Computer dialog, type **ClientXX**, click **Check Names**, and click **OK**.

20. Because there are no more options to configure, click **Next** until you get to the last screen and then click **Finish**. Review the possible options you can configure for this program on each screen.

21. After a moment, a report should appear in the right pane. Click **show all** on the Summary tab. Unfortunately, you will see different results than the Group Policy Results Wizard showed in Step 15. Group Policy Modeling Wizard shows that the MemberServers-Logon GPO would be applied to ClientXX but we already saw that it was not. This discrepancy lies in the fact that the WMI Filter is not correctly evaluated. If you look under WMI Filters you will see that the Server2008 filter evaluated to True. Generally, Group Policy Modeling can be used as a valuable 'what if' tool for GPO processing, but if your GPOs include WMI Filters, the results may not be entirely correct.

22. Now, let's clean things up a bit. Delete the **DevGPO** and **SwDeployUser** GPOs from the Development OU, and the **MemberServers-Logon** GPO from the MemberServers OU. Remember, deleting the GPO from the OU deletes only the link; it does not actually delete the GPO. Remove the Block Inheritance option from the Hardware OU. Then move ClientXX back to the MemberComputers OU.

23. Close all open windows on all computers and shut down ServerCoreXX and ClientXX. Leave Server1XX on if you are going on to the next chapter immediately. Otherwise, shut down Server1XX as well.

Review Questions

1. True or False? WMI Filters must be linked to a GPO before they are effective.

2. Besides WMI filtering, you can filter GPOs based on _____.

   a. User's First name, Last name, and Description

   b. Security group memberships

   c. User Account options

   d. Account expiration

3. Which of the following produces a report based on what policies have already been applied to a user and/or computer?

   a. Group Policy Modeling

   b. Group Policy Preferences

   c. Gpupdate

   d. Group Policy Results

4. True or False? You can associate only one WMI filter with a GPO.

5. Group Policy Management Console provides a 'what if' tool called _____.

INTRODUCTION TO WINDOWS NETWORKING

Labs included in this chapter

- Lab 8.1 Installing a Protocol Analyzer

- Lab 8.2 Working with Trace Route

- Lab 8.3 Understanding How ARP Works

Microsoft MCTS Exam #70-640 Objectives

Objective

The 70-640 objectives do not include Windows networking, but the content in this chapter has been presented to better prepare students to work with DNS and sites, both of which require an understanding of networking services and IP addressing.

Lab 8.1 Installing a Protocol Analyzer

Objectives

- Install the Wireshark protocol analyzer program
- Capture Ping (ICMP) and DNS packets

Materials Required

This lab requires the following:

- Server1XX
- ClientXX

Estimated completion time: **25 minutes**

Activity Background

Capturing and analyzing packets with a protocol analyzer can help you fully understand how a protocol works. A great deal of processing goes on behind the scenes of even simple network communications, and seeing the packets and their contents can help you fully grasp the networking process.

In this lab, you install a popular free protocol analyzer called Wireshark. With Wireshark, you can capture all packets that the NIC on your computer sees. In addition, you can create filters to see certain protocols or packets with certain addresses only. Once you install Wireshark on your server, you will ping your server from your client computer and capture the packets generated by the ping command.

Activity

1. Start Server1XX, if necessary, and log on as Administrator.

2. Start Internet Explorer, and go to the www.wireshark.org Web site. (If the Microsoft Phishing Filter starts, click **Ask me later** and click **OK**.) Click **Download Wireshark**. Depending upon whether you are running 32-bit Windows or 64-bit Windows, click the appropriate Windows Installer. Click **Save** when prompted. Choose Desktop as the download location. Click **Save**. Close **Internet Explorer**.

3. Once the download completes, click **Run**. Click **Run** again.

4. Once the Wireshark Setup program starts, click **Next**. Click **I Agree** on the License Agreement.

5. On the Choose Components screen, accept the defaults. Click **Next** on three successive screens.

6. On the Install WinPcap screen, make sure Install WinPcap is checked and click **Install**. On the WinPcap Installer screen, click **Next**. Click **Next**, click **I Agree**, and click **Install**. Click **Finish**. Click **Next**, and then click **Finish**.

7. To start Wireshark, click **Start**, click **All Programs**, and click **Wireshark**. Click to maximize the Wireshark program window if necessary.

8. In the Capture section of the screen, click **Capture Options**. In the Wireshark: Capture Options screen, make sure that the interface that is selected is your computer's Ethernet interface. You should be able to tell by the IP address that is displayed. If the correct interface is not selected, click the selection arrow and select the correct interface.

9. To capture all packets, accept the default and click the **Start** button. Unless there is no traffic on your network, you should be able to see some packets in a short time. If you don't see any packets, start Internet Explorer to generate some packets.

10. Once some packets have been captured, click the **Stop the running live capture** icon (fourth icon from the left—it has a red circle with an x in it).

11. The top half of the capture screen lists all the packets, one per row, that were captured. The information is summarized. Click any packet, and in the middle pane, you can click to expand each section of the packet. Figure 8-1 shows an HTTP packet selected with the TCP part of the packet displayed in the middle pane.

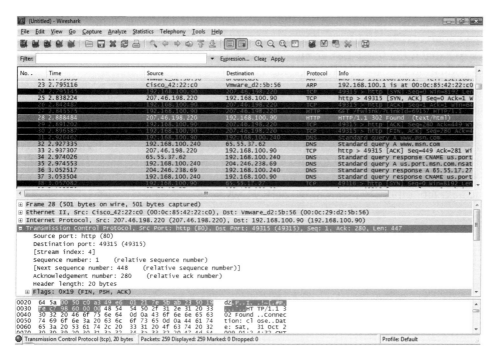

Figure 8-1 A packet capture in Wireshark

12. Start ClientXX and log on to the domain as Administrator (remember, you need to enter the user name as W2k8AD1XX\Administrator to logon to the domain). Open a command prompt. Type **ipconfig/ flushdns** and press **Enter** to clear the DNS cache. Next type **ping Server1XX** but do not press Enter yet.

13. On Server1XX, click the **Show the capture options** icon (second from the left). In the Wireshark: Capture Options screen, type **ip host 192.168.100.1XX** in the Capture Filter text box to specify all IP packets to or from Server1XX. Click **Start**. When prompted by Wireshark, if you wish to save the capture file, click **Continue without Saving**.

14. On ClientXX, press **Enter** at the command prompt. Once the ping completes, click the **Stop the running live capture** icon on Wireshark on Server1XX.

15. You should see a list of packets similar to Figure 8-2. The first packet is the DNS query from ClientXX and the second packet is the DNS response from Server1XX. The next eight packets are the ICMP request and reply packets (ping packets). Click the **DNS query** packet from ClientXX.

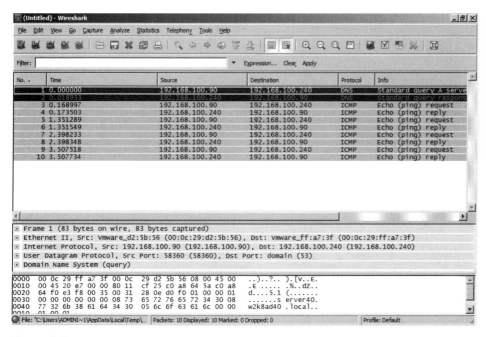

Figure 8-2 DNS and ICMP packets

16. In the middle pane, click to expand the line that begins with 'Ethernet II'; this data is the frame header. You will see the Destination and Source MAC addresses. The Internet Protocol line shows the source and destination IP addresses. Click to expand the **User Datagram Protocol** line. The source port is essentially a random number, but the destination port (53) is the port number for the DNS protocol.

17. Click to expand the **Domain Name System** (query) line. Then click to expand the **Queries** line and the line underneath. This part of the packet is what the DNS server gets; In this case, ClientXX is asking Server1XX to return the IP address of Server1XX.W2k8AD1XX.local.

18. Wireshark, and protocol analyzers like it, can capture packets to help you troubleshoot problems on a network. Close all open windows on Server1XX and ClientXX. When prompted by Wireshark if you wish to save the capture file, click **Quit without Saving**. Shut down ClientXX. Stay logged on to Server1XX if you are going on to the next lab; otherwise, shut down Server1XX.

Review Questions

1. True or False? To use a protocol analyzer to view packets sent between two systems, you must install the software on both systems.

2. Which protocol does the Ping program use to test network connectivity?

   a. UDP

   b. DNS

   c. ICMP

   d. TCP

3. When a computer queries a DNS server, which of the following is true?

   a. The UDP source port will always be 53.

   b. The TCP destination port will be a random number.

   c. The UDP destination port will always be 53.

   d. The ICMP destination port will always be 53.

4. True or False? When you ping a computer successfully from Windows, by default a total of eight ping packets are sent and received.

5. The frame header of a captured packet contains the source and destination _____ addresses.

Lab 8.2 Working with Trace Route

Objectives

- Use a protocol analyzer to inspect the packets generated by tracert

Materials Required

This lab requires the following:

- Server1XX

Estimated completion time: **10 minutes**

Activity Background

The tracert command relies on a feature of IP, called Time-to-live (TTL), to generate messages from each router that is in the path between the source and destination computers. In this lab, you will see how this process works by using a protocol analyzer to view each packet sent and received in a tracert session.

Activity

1. Log on to Server1XX as Administrator, if necessary.

2. Open a command prompt.

3. Start **Wireshark** and click **Capture Options**. In the Capture Filter text box, type **host Server1XX and icmp**. Click **Start**.

4. In the command prompt, type **tracert -d www.course.com**. The –d option in the command prevents tracert from trying to resolve host names. When the trace is complete, click the **Stop the running live capture** icon.

5. Click the first ICMP packet which should be an Echo request. Click to expand the **Internet Protocol** section in the middle pane. If necessary, scroll down to find the Time to live field. Your screen should look something like Figure 8-3.

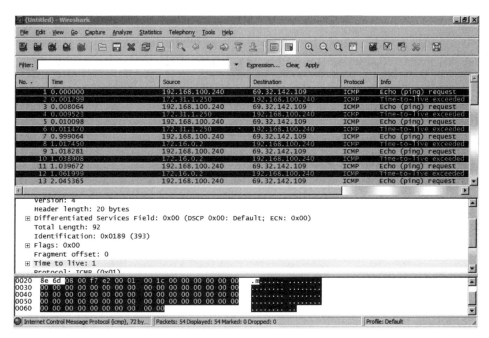

Figure 8-3 Capture of trace route

6. The Time-to-live (TTL) value is 1 in the first ICMP packet sent out by the tracert command. The TTL of a packet is decremented each time the packet reaches a router. When the TTL reaches 0, the router no longer will forward the packet and will instead send a TTL exceeded message back to the sending computer.

7. Click the second ICMP packet, which should have 'Time-to-live exceeded' in the Info column. The tracert command uses the information in the first TTL exceeded message to determine the address of the first router in the route between Server1XX and www.course.com.

8. Click the third ICMP packet and again view the TTL value. You will see that it is still 1. Tracert sends three packets with the same TTL value and displays the time it took to receive the replies. During times of slow response times, you can use this information to get an idea of which router in the path might be the bottleneck.

9. Click the seventh ICMP packet, which should be another Echo request. View the TTL on this packet, which should be 2. Tracert increments the TTL with each set of three packets, and each set of packets reaches the next router before the TTL becomes 0. When the TTL reaches 0, the router generates a TTL exceeded message. This sequence continues until the TTL is high enough to pass through all routers in the path and reach the destination device.

10. Scroll down until you reach the last set of packets, which should be three Echo requests that are each followed by an Echo reply from the final destination device.

11. Close all open windows on Server1XX. When prompted by Wireshark if you do not wish to save the capture file, click **Quit without Saving**.

Review Questions

1. What protocol is used by the tracert program?

   a. UDP

   b. ICMP

   c. TTL

   d. DNS

2. The –d option in the tracert command does which of the following?

   a. Prevents DNS lookups

   b. Causes host name resolution

   c. Causes the route to be deleted

   d. Causes the TTL to be set to 0

3. True or False? The TTL of a packet is incremented at each router.

4. True or False? A TTL exceeded message is generated when the TTL reaches 0.

5. The TTL field can be found in the _____ section of a packet.

Lab 8.3 Understanding How ARP Works

Objectives

- Use the ARP program to view and manage the ARP cache
- Capture and analyze ARP, ICMP, and DNS packets

Materials Required

This lab requires the following:

- Server1XX
- ClientXX

Estimated completion time: **20 minutes**

Activity Background

Computers use ARP to resolve known IP addresses to MAC addresses when the destination computer is on the same network as the source computer. Computers must also use ARP to determine the MAC address of their default gateway when they have a packet to send to a computer on another network.

The destination address of an ARP request packet is a broadcast address. The destination address of the ARP reply packet is a unicast address. When the source computer learns of another computer's MAC address via ARP, the source computer saves the address temporarily in its ARP cache so that it will not have to send an ARP broadcast each time it communicates with computers whose MAC address it already knows.

In this lab, you experiment with the ARP program and capture and analyze ARP, ICMP, and DNS packets.

Activity

1. Log on to Server1XX as Administrator, if necessary. Start ClientXX and log on to the domain as Administrator (remember, you need to enter the user name as W2k8AD1XX\Administrator to log on to the domain).

2. On Server1XX, open a command prompt. Type **arp -a** and press **Enter** to display the ARP cache. The information you see will depend upon how much communication with other computers your server has had recently. If ARP responds with 'No ARP Entries Found', type **ping clientXX** and press **Enter** and then **arp -a** and **Enter** again. You should see at least one entry.

3. Type **arp -d** and press **Enter** to clear the ARP cache. Start Wireshark. Click **Capture Options**. In the Capture Filter text box, type **host Server1XX and arp**. Then click **Start**.

4. On ClientXX, open a command prompt and type **arp -d** and press **Enter**. Type **ping Server1XX** and press **Enter**.

5. On Server1XX, stop the capture when the ping is complete. You should see four ARP packets in the capture window. Notice the first ARP packet is from ClientXX. The Info column says "Who has 192.168.100.1XX, tell 192.168.100.XX". ClientXX needs to get the MAC address from Server1XX before it can send the ping packets. The next ARP packet is the reply from Server1XX. Click the second packet and expand the **Address Resolution Protocol** line in the middle pane to get an idea of the content of an ARP reply.

6. The third and fourth ARP packets are Server1XX requesting the MAC address of ClientXX. Server1XX needs ClientXX's MAC address to reply to the ping packets. Click **Show the capture options**. This time, you will capture all arp packets in your network. In the Capture Filter box, type **arp and net 192.168.100.0/24**. Click **Start**, and then click **Continue without Saving**.

7. On ClientXX, type **arp -d** and press **Enter** to clear the ARP cache. Then type **ping 69.32.142.109** and press **Enter**. The IP address is the preceding sentence is the address of www.course.com. You don't want ClientXX to do a DNS lookup this time, so you are using the IP address.

8. On Server1XX, stop the capture. If there was no other ARP traffic on the network, you should see two ARP packets. (If there are other ARP packets, find the two ARP packets coming from and going to ClientXX.) Notice that the address that ClientXX used ARP to resolve was not the 69.32.142.109 address but was instead the address of the default gateway. When a computer needs to send a packet to a destination on another IP network, it has to send the packet to a router (default gateway). Therefore, it needs to get the MAC address of the default gateway, not the destination.

9. As the last example of using ARP, you capture all the packets involved in a simple ping. On ClientXX, type **arp -d**, press **Enter**, type **ipconfig/flushdns**, and press **Enter** to clear the DNS cache.

10. On Server1XX, open the Capture Options on Wireshark. In the Capture Filter, type **host Server1XX and (arp or icmp or port 53)**. This filter will cause Wireshark to capture all ARP, ICMP, and DNS packets coming from or going to Server1XX. Click **Start** and click **Continue without Saving**. Open a command prompt and type **arp -d** and press **Enter** to clear the ARP cache on Server1XX.

11. On ClientXX, type **ping Server1XX** and press **Enter**.

12. On Server1XX, stop the packet capture once the ping is finished. Scroll to the top of the list of packets if necessary. The sequence of packets you should see is as follows:

    • Two ARP packets—ClientXX is resolving the MAC address of its DNS server (in this case Server1XX)

    • One DNS packet—ClientXX is resolving the IP address of Server1XX

    • Two ARP packets—Server1XX is resolving the MAC address of ClientXX

    • One DNS packet—Server1XX is responding to ClientXX's DNS query

    • Eight ICMP packets (4 echo requests and 4 echo replies)

It is possible that the order above is not exactly what you see. Wireshark does not always display packets in the exact order in which they were generated. However, the above list displays the order in which the packets are generated by the two computers.

13. Close all open windows and shut down ClientXX. Shut down Server1XX only if you are not going on to the next chapter.

Review Questions

1. True or False? Before a data packet can be sent to another computer on the network, computers must use DNS to resolve the MAC address.

2. Which of the following is true about ARP?

   a. It is used to get the IP address of a computer.

   b. It is usually used after ICMP packets are sent by the ping command.

   c. It uses the broadcast address for the destination address of an ARP request.

   d. It must be used before every packet is sent.

3. Which of the following is true about the sequence of packets when the ping command is used and when the source computer's ARP and DNS caches are both empty?

   a. An ARP packet is usually the first packet.

   b. A DNS packet is usually the first packet.

   c. The DNS query destination address is a broadcast.

   d. The ARP request source address is a broadcast.

4. True or False? When a computer has the IP address of the destination computer in its ARP cache, it does not need to send a DNS query.

5. _____ is a protocol that resolves a known IP address to a MAC address.

CONFIGURING DNS FOR ACTIVE DIRECTORY

Labs included in this chapter

- Lab 9.1 Working with the DNS Cache and Capturing a Recursive DNS Lookup
- Lab 9.2 Working with the Global Names Zone
- Lab 9.3 Configuring Traditional and Conditional Forwarders
- Lab 9.4 Using Event and Debug Logging to Troubleshoot DNS

Microsoft MCTS Exam #70-640 Objectives

Objective	Lab
Configure DNS server settings	9.1

Lab 9.1 Working with the DNS Cache and Capturing a Recursive DNS Lookup

Objectives

- View and manage the DNS cache
- Capture DNS packets in a recursive lookup

Materials Required

This lab requires the following:

- Server1XX
- ClientXX

Estimated completion time: **15 minutes**

Activity Background

A recursive query is a DNS packet sent to a DNS server that requests the IP address of a computer given its name. When a DNS server is sent a recursive query, the DNS server attempts to resolve the query in this order:

1. From locally stored zone resource records
2. From the DNS cache
3. From conditional forwarders (if configured and the domain name matches)
4. From traditional forwarders (if configured)
5. Recursively by using root hints (only if no traditional forwarder is configured)

This lab gives you a detailed look at the process (with no forwarder configured) by capturing 1) the packets from the client making the query, 2) the packets sent to and from root and top-level domain servers, and 3) the packets sent to and from the name servers hosting the queried domain.

Activity

1. Start Server1XX if necessary and log on as Administrator. Start ClientXX and logon to the domain as Administrator.

2. On Server1XX, open DNS Manager: Click **Start**, **Administrative Tools**, and click **DNS**.

3. To work with the DNS cache, you must turn on Advanced view. Click **View** and click **Advanced**.

4. If you had a DNS server configured in your TCP/IP protocol configuration before you installed DNS, Windows Server 2008 would have installed it as a forwarder. If so, you want to delete it. Click **Server1XX** in the left pane and double-click **Forwarders** in the right pane to open Server1XX Properties with the Forwarders tab selected.

5. If an IP address is listed in the Forwarders tab, click **Edit**, click the **IP address**, and click **Delete**. Click **OK**. Click **OK** to close Server1XX Properties. If a forwarder is present, the DNS server will forward the query to the forwarder after checking its cache and let the forwarder continue the recursive query.

6. Expand **Server1XX**, if necessary, and expand **Cached Lookups**, **.(root)**, and then click **com**. You should see some folders and a list of NS server records that holds the names of the generic top-level domain (GTLD) servers. If the NS records are not present, the next step should cause them to be added to the cache. The GTLD servers are what the root servers return to the DNS server that makes a recursive lookup.

7. Right-click the **Cached Lookups** folder and click **Clear Cache**. All records are deleted except for the .(root) folder.

8. Open Internet Explorer and browse to **http://books.tomsho.com**. On this site, you will find resources for *MCTS Guide to Windows Server 2008 Active Directory Configuration* as well as this lab book. This action will also re-populate the DNS cache. Close Internet Explorer.

9. In DNS Manager, expand `.(root)` and click **com**. You will see the GTLD servers and a couple folders. These DNS records are cached from the DNS lookups required to load the books.tomsho.com Web site.

10. In the next steps, you will see exactly what was required of your DNS server to make that lookup. On ClientXX, open a command prompt. Type **nslookup** and press **Enter**. You only want IPv4 host records (A records), so type **set type=A** and press **Enter**.

11. On Server1XX, right-click the **Cached Lookups** folder and click **Clear Cache** again.

12. Start Wireshark, which you installed in Lab 8.1. Click **Capture Options**. In the Capture Filter text box, type **port 53** (the port for DNS) and click **Start**.

13. On ClientXX, at the nslookup prompt, type **books.tomsho.com** and press **Enter**.

14. On Server1XX, stop the capture. If all went well, you will see around 10 DNS records. Figure 9-1 shows the captured packets.

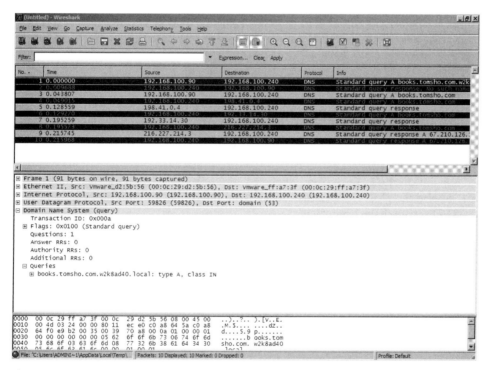

Figure 9-1 A recursive DNS lookup

15. Click the first captured packet. If necessary, scroll the window to the right to see the entire Info column. You should see that in the initial query, the client appended its own domain name onto books.tomsho.com, making the query books.tomsho.com.W2k8AD1XX.local. Appending the domain name is the default behavior (but you can change it on ClientXX if desired). The second packet shows that the response came back immediately from Server1XX, indicating that there was no such name in the W2k8AD1XX.local domain.

16. Click the third packet. This packet indicates a standard query for books.tomsho.com. In the middle pane, expand **Domain Name System** and expand **Flags**. You will see that the Recursion bit is set, indicating the query is to be recursive, as most client queries are.

17. Click the fourth packet, which is query from Server1XX to a different IP address. This IP address belongs to one of the root servers. Make a note of the IP address. Return to DNS Manager. Click **Server1XX** and double-click **Root Hints**. You should be able to find the IP address that Server1XX is querying. Click **Cancel**.

18. In Wireshark, expand **Flags** in the middle pane, if necessary. You will see that the Recursion flag is not set, indicating that the query is to be iterative, as most server to server queries are.

19. In Wireshark, click the fifth packet, which should be the response from the root server. In the middle pane, expand **Domain Name System** if necessary and expand **Authoritative nameservers**. You should see a list of GTLD servers. Your DNS server will query one of these in Step 20.

20. The sixth packet is a query to one of the GTLD servers returned by the root server. Click the seventh packet, which is the response by the GTLD server. You will see the name servers for the tomsho.com domain under Authoritative nameservers and their IP addresses under Additional records.

21. The eighth packet is the query to the nameserver responsible for the tomsho.com domain. Click the ninth packet. Expand **Answers**, if necessary and you see the returned address for books.tomsho.com. The last packet is Server1XX's response to ClientXX.

22. Start a new Wireshark capture by clicking the **Start a new live capture** icon (third icon from the left), and then click **Continue without Saving**.

23. On ClientXX, press the up arrow to repeat the last command in the command prompt and press **Enter**.

 Dnslookup does not check the local DNS cache before sending a query. However, if you were testing by using ping or a Web browser, you would need to flush your local DNS cache by typing ipconfig / flushdns and then pressing Enter.

24. On Server1XX, stop the capture. As you can see, only four DNS packets were generated this time. Only four were generated because DNS has cached the information for books.tomsho.com, and a recursive query need not be done because Server1XX has the information saved in its cache. Close Wireshark and click **Quit without Saving**.

25. In DNS Manager, expand **Cached Lookups**, **.(root)** and **com**. Click the **tomsho** folder. You will see the Name Server (NS) and the Host (A) records cached from the recent lookup. In the com folder, you will also see that the GTLD servers have been cached.

26. Close all open windows on ClientXX and ServerXX. Stay logged on to Server1XX and ClientXX if you are going on to the next lab; otherwise, shut down both machines.

Review Questions

1. True or False? To properly test DNS using nslookup, you should clear your client's local DNS cache using ipconfig /flushdns.

2. When a DNS server receives a recursive query, what is the second step in resolving the query (assuming the first step did not provide a successful result)?

    a. Check the DNS cache

    b. Check if the domain name is part of the local zone data

    c. Query a root server

    d. Query a top-level domain server

3. When a DNS server has a forwarder configured, which of the following is true?

    a. The DNS server sends the query to the forwarder after getting a negative reply from the root servers.

    b. The DNS server immediately sends the query to the forwarder without checking its zone data or cache.

    c. The query is sent to the forwarder but the DNS server continues the recursive query and uses the best result.

    d. The query is sent to the forwarder and the root servers are not queried.

4. True or False? Root servers reply with the name and address of authoritative name servers for the domain being queried.

5. The type of query sent from a DNS client to a DNS server is usually a(n) _____ query.

Lab 9.2 Working with the Global Names Zone

Objectives

- Configure the Global Names Zone feature in DNS

Materials Required

This lab requires the following:

- Server1XX
- ClientXX

Estimated completion time: **10 minutes**

Activity Background

Although WINS still is supported in Windows Server 2008 and Vista, Windows Server 2008 includes a new feature to help IT administrators migrate away from WINS. This new feature, the GlobalNames Zone (GNZ), provides a method for IT administrators to add single-label names (computer names that don't use a domain suffix) to DNS, thereby allowing client computers to resolve these names without knowing the correct DNS suffix for the host being queried. The GNZ is not a replacement for a dynamically created WINS database because records in this zone must be added manually. For important servers with names currently being resolved by WINS, however, a GNZ is an option worth considering, especially if only a few hosts are the sole reason for maintaining WINS.

GNZ functionality is not just a partial replacement for WINS, however. If your network supports mobile users whose laptops and other mobile devices are unlikely to have the correct DNS suffixes configured, GNZ can make access to servers these users need more convenient. That is, instead of mobile users having to remember resource FQDNs, they can access them by using a single-label name, such as Web1.

In this lab, you enable and configure the GNZ feature.

Activity

1. Log on to Server1XX as Administrator, if necessary. Open a command prompt. To enable GlobalNames Zone (GNZ) support, type **dnscmd Server1XX /config /EnableGlobalNamesSupport 1** and press **Enter**. Close the command prompt. If you had multiple DNS servers, you would need to run the command for each server.

2. Open DNS Manager. Right-click **Server1XX** and click **New Zone**. The New Zone Wizard starts. Click **Next**.

3. In the Zone Type screen, select **Primary zone** and **Store the zone in Active Directory**, if necessary. Click **Next.**

4. In the Active Directory Zone Replication Scope screen, accept the default of To all DNS servers in this domain and click **Next**.

5. In the Forward or Reverse Lookup Zone screen, accept the default of Forward lookup zone and click **Next**.

6. In the Zone name text box, type **GlobalNames** and click **Next**. On the Dynamic Update screen, click **Do not allow dynamic updates** and click **Next**. Click **Finish**.

7. Expand **Forward Lookup Zones** and click **GlobalNames**.

8. In the right pane, right-click in empty space and click **New Alias (CNAME)**. In the Alias name text box, type **MyClient**. Click the **Browse** button.

9. In the Browse screen, double-click **Server1XX** and double-click **Forward Lookup Zones**. Double-click **W2k8AD1XX.local** and click **ClientXX**. Click **OK**. Click **OK** again.

10. Click **GlobalNames** if necessary. You will see the Alias (CNAME) record you just created.

11. From ClientXX, log on to the domain as **Administrator**. Open a command prompt.

12. Type **nslookup myclient** and press **Enter**. You should get a response with the FQDN of ClientXX and its IP Address. See Figure 9-2.

Figure 9-2   Results from nslookup myclient after GlobalNames zone setup

13. The GlobalNames zone feature is not very useful when you have a single domain. However, it is useful when you have multiple domains and sub-domains and want clients to be able to access any host in the forest using only its host name. The GlobalNames Zone feature allows clients to use just the host name of the server they want to access rather than the FQDN when the server is not in the same domain as the client. Close all open windows on Server1XX and ClientXX.

14. Shut down ClientXX. Stay logged on to Server1XX if you are going on to the next lab; otherwise, shut down Server1XX.

Review Questions

1. What type of records do you create in the GlobalNames Zone?

    a. A

    b. AAAA

    c. CNAME

    d. SRV

2. What type of zone is a GlobalNames Zone?

    a. Reverse lookup

    b. Secondary

    c. Forward lookup

    d. Stub

3. True or False? The GlobalNames feature does not support dynamic DNS updates.

4. True or False? To successfully query a host using a single name, clients must be in the same domain as the actual host that is referenced in the GlobalNames Zone.

5. To enable the GlobalNames feature for a server named DNSServ1, you must type _____.

Lab 9.3 Configuring Traditional and Conditional Forwarders

Objectives

- Configure a traditional forwarder
- Configure a conditional forwarder

Materials Required

This lab requires the following:

- Server1XX

Estimated completion time: **20 minutes**

Activity Background

A traditional forwarder is a DNS server to which other DNS servers send requests that they themselves cannot resolve. A forwarder is commonly used when a DNS server on an internal, private network receives a query for a domain on the public Internet. The internal DNS server forwards the request recursively to a DNS server connected to the public Internet. This method prevents the internal DNS server from having to contact root servers and TLD servers directly, thereby shielding internal servers from the public Internet.

A conditional forwarder is a DNS server to which other DNS servers send requests targeted for a specific domain. For example, computers in the coolgadgets.com domain might send a DNS query for a computer named server1.niftytools.com. The DNS server in the coolgadgets.com domain can be configured with a conditional forwarder that in effect says "If you receive a query for niftytools.com, forward it to the DNS server handling the niftytools.com domain."

Servers that are forwarders or conditional forwarders require no special configuration, but the servers using them as forwarders must be configured to do so.

In this lab, you first perform some DNS lookups without forwarders configured and inspect the results. Then you configure a traditional forwarder and see how the results differ. Finally, you configure a conditional forwarder.

Activity

1. Log on to Server1XX as Administrator, if necessary. Start DNS Manager.

2. In DNS Manager, click **Server1XX**. Right-click **Cached Lookups** and click **Clear Cache**. Expand **Cached Lookups, .(root)** and any other folders you see under Cached Lookups. The only resource record you are likely to see is an A record for localhost, which is read from the Hosts file.

3. Open a command prompt and type **nslookup www.course.com** and press **Enter**. You should get a response giving that address for course.com.

4. In DNS Manager, click the **Refresh** icon. Expand **Cached Lookups** and **.(root)**. You should see a few folders underneath the .(root) folder, including a folder named com. Click the **com** folder to view the .com domains that have been cached by doing the nslookup in Step 3. You should also see a list of gtld-servers that were returned when your DNS server queried a root server.

5. Right-click **Server1XX** and click **Properties**. Click the **Forwarders** tab, and click **Edit**.

6. In the Edit Forwarders dialog box, type the IP address of the classroom DNS server, if available, and press **Enter**. If you do not know of a DNS server address you can use, type **198.60.121.5** and press **Enter**. Click **OK**. Click **OK** again.

7. Right-click **Cached Lookups** and click **Clear Cache**. From a command prompt, type **nslookup www. course.com** and press **Enter**. You should get a response that includes the IP address for www.course.com.

8. Refresh the display in DNS Manager. Expand **Cached Lookups**, and **.(root)** and click the **com** folder. You still see a few folders of records that were retrieved by the www.course.com lookup; however, what you don't see is the list of gtld-servers. The gtld-servers are not cached because they were never queried by this server. Once your DNS server determined it did not have the record for www.course.com in its zone data or in its cache, it forwarded the request to the address you typed in the Forwarders tab in Step 6. Then, it just waited for the forwarder to finish the query and return the reply for www.course.com.

9. Repeat Steps 7 and 8, except this time use www.microsoft.com or another domain of your choice. You will find that you get similar results.

10. To delete the forwarder, right-click **Server1XX**, and click **Properties**. Click the **Forwarders** tab and click **Edit**. Click the **IP address** and click **Delete**. Click **OK** twice.

11. Right-click the **Conditional Forwarders** folder in the left pane and click **New Conditional Forwarder**.

12. In the DNS Domain box, type **tomsho.com**. In the IP addresses of the master servers box, type the address you used in Step 6 and press **Enter**. Click **OK**. This causes any queries for the tomsho.com domain to be forwarded to the specified IP address. (Normally, you would use an authoritative name server for the specified domain, but the result is the same.)

13. At the command prompt, type **nslookup books.tomsho.com** and press **Enter**. You should get a reply. If you do not get a reply, review Steps 11 and 12 to verify you have entered the information correctly.

14. In DNS Manager, check the com folder in the Cached Lookups folder to verify that no gtld-servers have been cached.

15. From the command prompt again, type **nslookup www.course.com** and press **Enter**. Check the DNS cache again in DNS Manager. You should see that the gtld-servers have been cached by that lookup. Thus, as you can see, a conditional forwarder forwards requests only for particular domains while a traditional forwarder forwards all requests that can't be resolved from the DNS server's zone data or cache. You can have both conditional and traditional forwarders configured on a DNS server. The DNS server will first check if the queried domain is in the list of conditional forwarders and, if not, then send the request to a traditional forwarder.

16. Now you need to delete the conditional forwarder. Click **Conditional Forwarders**, right-click **tomsho.com,** and click **Delete**. Click **Yes**. Close all open windows.

17. Stay logged on to Server1XX if you are going to the next lab; otherwise, shut down Server1XX.

Review Questions

1. True or False? A list of Gtld-servers is returned as a result of a query to root servers.

2. Which of the following is true when a traditional forwarder is configured?

   a. Root servers are not queried if a forwarder can be contacted.

   b. Gtld-servers are returned by the configured forwarder.

   c. All queries to the DNS server are sent to the forwarder.

   d. Only queries for specific domains are sent to traditional forwarders.

3. Which of the following is true about conditional and traditional forwarders?

   a. You can configure either conditional or traditional forwarders, but not both.

   b. Conditional forwarders are checked for a matching domain before traditional forwarders are queried.

   c. All queries are sent to the conditional forwarder if the query can't be resolved from the local zone data.

   d. When a traditional forwarder is configured but cannot be contacted, the DNS server always sends a failure reply to the client making the query.

4. True or False? A list of root servers is returned as a result of a query to a gtld-server.

5. To have a DNS server send queries to another DNS server when a specific domain is queried, you should configure a(n) _____.

Lab 9.4 Using Event and Debug Logging to Troubleshoot DNS

Objectives

- View DNS Event Logging options and view the DNS event log
- Enable Debug Logging and view the contents of a debug log file

Materials Required

This lab requires the following:

- Server1XX
- ClientXX

Estimated completion time: **20 minutes**

Activity Background

When DNS is installed, a new event log is created to record informational, error, and warning events generated by the DNS server. In the Event Logging tab of the server's Properties dialog box, you configure which event types should be logged. Events you're likely to find in the DNS Server log include zone serial number changes, zone transfer requests, and DNS server startup and shutdown events. When DNS problems are evident and misconfigurations make them difficult to trace, the event log is the first place to look for causes and solutions.

When serious DNS debugging is warranted, you can enable debug logging in the server's Properties dialog box. Debug logging will record in a text file selected packets coming from and going to the DNS server. The first part of the file is a key to help you interpret the captured data. Each line of the file—starting with date and time—is a summary of a captured packet. If necessary, you can enable logging of detailed packet contents.

In this lab, you view the options available for event and debug logging.

Activity

1. Log on to Server1XX as Administrator, if necessary. Start DNS Manager.

2. In DNS Manager, right-click **Server1XX** and click **Properties**. Click the **Event Logging** tab. Notice that the default setting is for All events to be logged. "All events" include DNS server stops and starts as well as any warnings or errors that might indicate a misconfigured or malfunctioning DNS server. These events can be viewed using Event Viewer.

3. Leave Server1XX Properties open. To view recent DNS events, start **Server Manager**, expand **Roles**, and click **DNS Server**. In the Summary section, you will see an Events window showing only events for DNS Server. Viewing events for a particular server role in Server Manager is frequently easier than navigating the Event Viewer.

4. For comparison, click **Go to Event Viewer**. In the left pane, expand **Event Viewer** and expand **Applications and Services Logs**. Click **DNS Server** under Applications and Services Logs. You will see the same information you viewed in Step 3. Close Server Manager.

5. On the Server Properties screen, click the **Debug Logging** tab.

6. Click **Log packets for debugging**. In the File path and name text box, type **c:\dnslog.txt**. You will see a screen similar to Figure 9-3. Examine the options available for debug logging. Accept the rest of the default settings and click **OK**. Clear the DNS cache by right-clicking **Cached Lookups** and clicking **Clear Cache**.

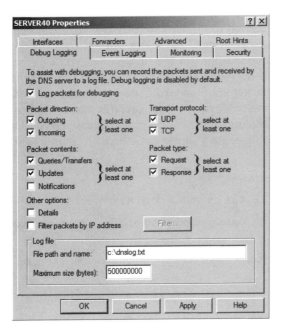

Figure 9-3   DNS Debug Logging tab

7. Start ClientXX and log on to the domain as **Administrator**. Open a command prompt and type **nslookup www.microsoft.com** and press **Enter**.

8. On Server1XX in DNS Manager, right-click **Server1XX** and point to **All Tasks** and click **Stop**. (By stopping the DNS server, the DNS debugging file will be closed and will flush the data waiting to be written to it.)

9. Click **Start**, click **Computer**, and double-click the **C:** drive. Double-click **dnslog.txt** to open the debugging file. You should see a file similar to Figure 9-4.

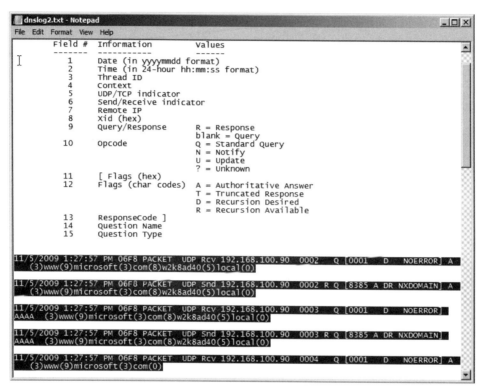

Figure 9-4   DNS debug log

10. The highlighted lines in Figure 9-4 are the lines that pertain to the lookup for www.microsoft.com. (There were a number of records before these lines that have been edited out.) You can decipher the contents of each packet by using the key at the top of the file. For example, in the first packet, you can see that the code *Rcv* means that the packet was received by the DNS server and that 192.168.100.90 was the address of the sending computer. The *Q* code means that the packet is a Standard Query. In brackets, the *0001* code followed by *D* indicates a recursive query. After the brackets, the *A* code indicates that an A (host) record was being queried. At the end of the packet is the host name that was queried. Review the contents of the log file until you are comfortable deciphering its contents. As you can see, there are quite a few packets involved with a single DNS query. Close the log file.

11. In Windows Explorer, delete **dnslog.txt**.

12. In DNS Manager, right-click **Server1XX**, point to **All Tasks** and click **Start** to restart the DNS server.

13. Right-click **Server1XX**, and click **Properties**. Click **Debug Logging** and click **Log packets for debugging** to disable debug logging. Click **OK**.

14. Close **DNS Manager**. Log off and shut down ClientXX and Server1XX unless you are going on immediately to the next chapter.

Review Questions

1. True or False? Debug Logging is enabled by default while Event Logging is disabled by default.

2. Which of the following is *not* an option for Event Logging?

   a. Errors only

   b. All events

   c. Warnings only

   d. Errors and warnings

3. Which of the following is true about Debug Logging?

   a. You can choose which transport protocols you wish to log.

   b. You can choose which DNS ports should be logged.

   c. By default, packet details are logged when you enable debug logging.

   d. The log file is always stored in C:\Windows\DNS\Logging.

4. True or False? The DNS Debug Logging file shows whether a packet was sent or received.

5. If you want Debug Logging to log only those packets coming from or going to particular computers, you should click the _____ option.

9

CONFIGURING AND MAINTAINING THE ACTIVE DIRECTORY INFRASTRUCTURE

Labs included in this chapter

- Lab 10.1 Installing a New Domain Controller in a New Forest
- Lab 10.2 Create an External Trust
- Lab 10.3 Testing an External Trust
- Lab 10.4 Working with Operations Masters

Microsoft MCTS Exam #70-640 Objectives

Objective	Lab
Configuring the Active Directory Infrastructure	10.1
Configure DNS server settings	10.2, 10.3
Configure trusts	10.2, 10.3
Maintain Active Directory accounts	10.3
Configure operations masters	10.4
Configure a forest or domain	10.4

Lab 10.1 Installing a New Domain Controller in a New Forest

Objectives

- Install a new domain controller
- Test cross-forest access before a trust is configured

Materials Required

This lab requires the following:

- Server1XX
- Server2XX

Estimated completion time: **15 minutes**

Activity Background

An external trust is a one-way or two-way nontransitive trust between two domains that aren't in the same forest that allows security principals in the trusted domain to access resources in the trusting domain. A forest trust is a one-way or two-way transitive trust between forests that allows security principals in the trusted forest to access resources in any domain in the trusting forest. In order for you to work with external and forest trusts, you need to configure a new domain controller in a new forest. In this activity, you install Active Directory on a server named Server2XX to make it a domain controller in a new forest. You will verify that in order to access resources in that remote forest, you need to log on separately to the domain in the remote forest.

Activity

1. Start Server1XX. Start and log on to Server2XX as Administrator using **Password01**. Change the Administrator password to **Password02**. Press **Ctrl+Alt+Del** and click **Change a password**. In the Old password box, type **Password01**, and in the New password and Confirm password boxes, type **Password02**. Click the arrow and then click **OK**.

2. On Server2XX, start Server Manager. Click **Roles**, and then click **Add Roles**.

3. In the Add Roles Wizard, click **Next**. Click **Active Directory Domain Services** and click **Next**. Click **Next** and then click **Install**.

4. On the Installation Results screen, click **Close this wizard and launch the Active Directory Domain Services Installation Wizard (dcpromo.exe)**.

5. On the Active Directory Domain Services Installation Wizard screen, click **Next**, and then click **Next**. Click **Create a new domain in a new forest** and click **Next**.

6. On the Name the Forest Root Domain screen, type **W2k8AD2XX.local** and click **Next**.

7. On the Set Forest Functional Level screen, click the selection arrow and click **Windows Server 2008**. Click **Next**.

8. On the Additional Domain Controller Options screen, accept the defaults and click **Next**. You may receive a message stating "This computer has dynamically assigned IP addresses." You see this message because your IPv6 protocol is using dynamic addresses by default. Click **Yes, the computer will use a dynamically assigned IP address**.

9. If you receive a message stating that a delegation for this DNS server cannot be created, click **Yes**. Click **Next**. In the Directory Services Restore Mode Administrator Password screen, type **Password02** twice and click **Next**. Click **Next**.

10. When the installation completes, click **Finish**. Click **Restart Now** when prompted.

11. Once Server2XX restarts, log on as **Administrator** using **Password02**.

12. By default, when you install Active Directory Domain Services and DNS together, any DNS server that was configured in your IP address settings is added as a forwarder. You don't want the forwarder configured at

this time. Open **DNS Manager**. Click the **Server2XX** node in DNS Manager. In the right pane, double-click **Forwarders**. Click **Edit**. Click the **IP address** you see and click **Delete**. Then click **OK** twice.

13. Just as a test, try to access Server1XX. Click **Start** and type **\\Server1XX** in the Start Search box and press **Enter**. Server2XX does not have any DNS information for Server1XX, so you get a Network Error message.

14. Now you will try using the IP address of Server1XX. Click **Start** and type **\\192.168.100.1XX** in the Start Search box and press **Enter**.

15. You should get a Connect to dialog box. In the User name box, type **Administrator**, and then type **Password02** in the Password box. Click **OK**. You should get a message stating the logon was unsuccessful. In the User name box, type **W2k8AD1XX\Administrator**, and in the Password box, type **Password01** and click **OK**. This time, you should be successful and should see a list of the shares available on Server1XX. Close Windows Explorer.

16. To access resources on a computer in a remote forest, it is necessary to logon using an account that is valid in the remote forest. In the next lab, you will create an external trust between the domains forest W2k8AD1XX and W2k8AD2XX, thereby allowing you to log on to the W2k8AD2XX forest and access resources in the W2k8AD1XX forest. Stay logged on to Server1XX and Server2XX if you are going to the next lab; otherwise, shut down both machines.

Review Questions

1. True or False? When you install Active Directory Domain Services, the option to install DNS is selected by default.

2. Which of the following is an option when installing Active Directory Domain Services? (Choose all that apply.)

    a. Add a domain controller to an existing domain

    b. Create a new domain in a new forest

    c. Create a new forest in an existing domain

    d. Add a domain to an existing domain controller

3. Which of the following is true when you have more than one forest in a network?

    a. You can access resources in a remote forest as long as the user name you log on with in your forest is the same as a valid user name in the remote forest.

    b. You must log on to the remote forest using a valid user name and password for the remote forest.

    c. As long as the two forests are on the same network, they have a built-in trust between them.

    d. You cannot log on to a forest remotely; you must log on to a computer that is a member of a domain in the forest to access resources.

4. True or False? The first domain controller in a new forest cannot be a global catalog server.

5. In DNS, a(n) _____ is configured automatically when you install AD DS and DNS together.

Lab 10.2 Create an External Trust

Objectives

- Configure DNS for an external trust
- Create an external trust

Materials Required

This lab requires the following:

- Server1XX
- Server2XX

Estimated completion time: **30 minutes**

Activity Background

External trusts are configured in Active Directory Domains and Trusts. An external trust is created between domains in different forests or between domains in a Windows Server 2003/2008 forest and a Windows 2000 Server forest or Windows NT domain. Recall that Windows 2000 Server and Windows NT don't support forest trusts, so an external trust is the only way to build a trust relationship between forests in these OSs and Windows Server 2003/2008 forests. A significant difference between an external trust and a forest trust is that with an external trust, the trust exists only between the specified domains. With a forest trust, the trust exists between all the domains in both forests. In this lab, you create a one-way external trust between the domains W2k8AD1XX.local and W2k8AD2XX.local.

As part of creating external trusts, you must also configure DNS settings in both forests so that the domain controllers can find one another. The options for DNS configuration for this purpose include conditional forwarders, stub zones, and secondary zones. In this lab, you will configure a stub zone on Server1XX pointing to the W2k8AD2XX.local domain and a secondary zone on Server2XX; the secondary zone will hold the contents of the W2k8AD1XX.local domain. For full DNS operation, reverse lookup zones must also be functional; thus, you will create one for the W2k8AD1XX.local domain.

Activity

1. Log on to Server1XX as Administrator, if necessary. Log on to Server2XX as Administrator, if necessary.

2. On Server1XX, open DNS Manager. Expand **Server1XX**.

3. Before you create the stub zone for Server2XX, a reverse lookup zone should be created for full DNS functionality. Click **Reverse Lookup Zones**, and then right-click **Reverse Lookup Zones** and click **New Zone**. Click **Next**. On the Zone Type screen, accept the defaults and click **Next**. On the Active Directory Zone Replication Scope screen, click **Next**. On the Reverse Lookup Zone Name screen, click **Next**, and in the Network ID box, type **192.168.100**. Click **Next**. Click **Next**. Click **Finish**.

4. To add Server1XX to the reverse lookup zone, click to expand **Forward Lookup Zones** and then click the **W2k8AD1XX.loca**l folder and double-click **Server1XX**. Click the **Update associated pointer (PTR) record** option. Click **OK**. Under Reverse Lookup Zones, click **100.168.192.in-addr.arpa** and click the **Refresh** icon. You will see the PTR record for Server1XX.

5. Create a reverse lookup zone record for Server2XX. Under Reverse Lookup Zones, right-click **100.168.192.in-addr.arpa** and click **New Pointer (PTR)**.

6. In the New Resource Record dialog box, type **2XX** in the Host IP Address field. The text in the Fully qualified domain name (FQDN) field changes to 2XX.100.168.192.in-addr.arpa. In the Host name field, type **Server2XX.W2k8AD2XX.local**. Click **OK**.

7. Click **Forward Lookup Zones** and then right-click **Forward Lookup Zones** and click **New Zone**. In the New Zone Wizard's welcome window, click **Next**.

8. In the Zone Type window, click the **Stub zone** option button, check the **Store the zone in Active Directory** check box, if necessary, and then click **Next**.

9. In the Active Directory Zone Replication Scope window, click **To all DNS servers in this domain**, if necessary, and then click **Next**. (If you had multiple domains, you might want to choose To all DNS servers in this forest.)

10. In the Zone name text box, type **W2k8AD2XX.local**, and then click **Next**.

11. In the Master DNS Servers window, type the IP address of Server2XX (**192.168.100.2XX**) and press **Enter**. Click **Next**, and then click **Finish**.

12. In DNS Manager, expand **Forward Lookup Zones**, if necessary, and then double-click the **W2k8AD2XX.local** zone to verify that SOA, NS, and A records are present.

13. To test the stub zone, open a command prompt window, type **nslookup W2k8AD2XX.local**, and press **Enter**. The IP addresses of all DNS servers for the W2k8AD2XX.local domain are displayed. Close the command prompt window.

14. On Server2XX, open DNS Manager. Expand **Server2XX**, and then click **Forward Lookup Zones**. Right-click **Forward Lookup Zones** and click **New Zone**. Click **Next**.

15. In the Zone Type window, click **Secondary zone**. Notice how the option to store the zone in Active Directory becomes grayed out because you cannot store a secondary zone in Active Directory. Click **Next**.

16. In the Zone name box, type **W2k8AD1XX.local** and click **Next**.

17. In the Master DNS Servers window, type the IP address of Server1XX (**192.168.100.1XX**) and press **Enter**. Click **Next**, click **Next**, and then click **Finish**.

18. The secondary zone will not contain any records. Click **W2k8AD1XX.local** and you see a message stating that the zone was not loaded. You need to configure zone transfers on Server1XX for zone transfers to occur.

19. On Server1XX, in DNS Manager, right-click the **W2k8AD1XX.local** zone and click **Properties**.

20. Click the **Zone Transfers** tab. Click **Allow zone transfers**. Click **Only to servers listed on the Name Servers tab**. Click **Apply**. You will make Server2XX a name server for this zone because it will hold a secondary copy of the zone information.

21. Click the **Name Servers** tab. Click **Add**. In the Server fully qualified domain name (FQDN) box, type **Server2XX.W2k8AD2XX.local** and click **Resolve**. The IP address for Server2XX should appear. Click **OK**. Don't worry if there is a message next to the address stating that the address is not authoritative for the zone. That message will clear itself in several minutes. Click **OK**.

22. On Server2XX, in DNS Manager, click **W2k8AD1XX.local** and click **Refresh**. If the zone data has not yet been transferred, right-click **W2k8AD1XX.local** and click **Transfer from Master**. You should see all the zone data from the W2k8AD1XX.local zone.

23. To test your secondary zone, open a command prompt window, type **nslookup W2k8AD1XX.local**, and press **Enter**. The IP address of Server1XX is displayed.

24. Close all open windows on both servers.

25. On Server1XX, open Active Directory Domains and Trusts. Right-click **W2k8AD1XX.local** and click **Properties**.

26. Click the **Trusts** tab, and click the **New Trust** button to start the New Trust Wizard. Click **Next** in the wizard's welcome window.

27. Type **W2k8AD2XX.local** in the Name text box, and then click **Next**.

28. The External trust option button is selected by default. Click **Next**.

29. In the Direction of Trust window, click **One-way: outgoing**, and then click **Next**.

30. In the Sides of Trust window, click **Both this domain and the specified domain**. If you're creating only one side of the trust, you're asked to enter a trust password, which must be used to create the second side of the trust. Click **Next**.

31. Type **administrator** in the User name text box and **Password02** in the Password text box, and then click **Next**. (If you enter incorrect credentials, you must restart the trust creation process.)

32. In the Outgoing Trust Authentication Level—Local Domain window, select **Domain-wide authentication**, if necessary, for the authentication level, and then click **Next**.

33. Review your settings in the Trust Selections Complete window, and then click **Next**.

34. In the Trust Creation Complete window, the status of the trust creation and a summary of your choices are displayed. Click **Next**.

35. In the Confirm Outgoing Trust window, click **Yes, confirm the outgoing trust**, and then click **Next**.

36. Click **Finish**. You get a message about SID filtering. Click **OK**. The Trusts tab lists W2k8AD2XX.local in the outgoing trusts lists. Click **OK**. Close all open windows on Server1XX.

37. On Server2XX, open Active Directory Domains and Trusts. Right-click **W2k8AD2XX.local** and click **Properties**. Click the **Trusts** tab. Notice that W2k8AD1XX.local is listed in the incoming trusts list. Click **OK**.

38. Stay logged on to Server1XX and Server2XX if you are going on to the next lab; otherwise, shut down both machines.

Review Questions

1. Which of the following is true about a secondary zone?

   a. Replication occurs automatically; there is no need to configure it.

   b. Secondary zones are read-only.

   c. Secondary zones can be Active Directory-integrated.

   d. Secondary zones contain only SOA and NS records.

2. Which of the following is true about stub zones?

   a. A stub zone is the only suitable zone type for domain resolution when a forest or external trust is needed.

   b. Stub zones are read-only zones.

   c. A stub zone contains only SOA, NS, and glue A records.

   d. Stub zones cannot be Active Directory-integrated.

3. True or False? An external trust can be created between a Windows domain and a non-Windows OS.

4. True or False? External trusts are not transitive.

5. If you want a zone to contain only SOA, NS, and glue A records for a primary zone, and you want the zone data to update automatically, you should create a _____ zone.

Lab 10.3 Testing an External Trust

Objectives

- Add users from a trusted domain to a group
- Test cross-forest access to resources

Materials Required

This lab requires the following:

- Server1XX
- Server2XX

Estimated completion time: **20 minutes**

Activity Background

An external trust permits accounts in the trusted domain to be added to groups and permissions lists in the trusting domain. In a one-way trust, one domain is called the trusted domain and the other domain is called the trusting domain. With a one-way trust, accounts in the trusted domain can access resources in the trusting domain, but not vice versa. In this lab you will test the external trust you created in Lab 10.2.

Activity

1. Log on to Server2XX as Administrator, if necessary.

2. Click **Start**, type **\\Server1XX.W2k8AD1XX.local** and press **Enter**. A Windows Explorer window should open that lists all shares on Server1XX.

3. Double-click **W2k8Shares**, which is the DFS root you created in Lab 6.4. It should open because the share has Read permission assigned to the Everyone group, which includes authenticated users from other forests. Note, however, that you did not have to enter credentials to see the list of shares or access this share as you did in Lab 10.1. Close the Explorer window.

4. Log on to Server1XX as **Administrator**, if necessary.

5. Click **Start**, click **Computer**, and double-click the **Data1** volume. Right-click, point to **New**, and click **Folder** and type **TestTrust** for the folder name.

6. Right-click **TestTrust** and click **Properties**. Click the **Sharing** tab. Click **Advanced Sharing**.

7. On the Advanced Sharing dialog box, click **Share this folder**. Click **Permissions**. Click **Add**.

8. In the Select Users, Computers, or Groups dialog box, type **Administrators** and click **Check Names**. Click **OK**. In the Share Permissions list box, Administrators (W2k8AD1XX\Administrators) is added. Check the **Full Control** check box in the Allow column of the Permissions for Administrator list box. Click **Everyone** and click **Remove** and then click **OK** twice.

9. Click the **Security** tab. Click **Administrators** in the Group or user names box and verify that Administrators has Full Control. Click **Users** and verify that Users has Read & execute, List folder contents, and Read permissions. Click **Close**. Close all open windows on Server1XX.

10. On Server2XX, click **Start** and type **\\Server1XX.W2k8AD1XX.local** and press **Enter**.

11. Double-click **TestTrust** in the Explorer window. You should get an error message indicating Windows cannot access the share. Click **Diagnose**. You should get a message indicating that the account you are logged on with was denied access. Click **Cancel**.

12. On Server1XX, open Active Directory Users and Computers. Expand **W2k8AD1XX.local** if necessary. Click **Builtin**. Double-click **Administrators** to open its Properties dialog box.

13. On Administrators Properties, click **Members**. Click **Add**. In the Select Users, Contacts, Computers, or Groups dialog box, click **Locations**. In the Locations box, click **W2k8AD2XX.local** and click **OK**. Note that if there was no trust between the domains, you would not be able to select W2k8AD2XX.local.

14. In the Enter the object names to select box, type **administrator** and click **Check Names**.

15. In the Enter Network Password screen, type **administrator@W2k8AD1XX.local** in the User name box and **Password02** in the Password box. Click **OK** three times.

16. On Server2XX, log off and log back on as **Administrator**. Click **Start** and type **\\Server1XX.W2k8AD1XX.local** and press **Enter**.

17. By adding the W2k8AD2XX.local Administrator account to the Administrators group on W2k8AD1XX.local, you have successfully granted that account administrator access to the W2k8AD1XX.local domain. Double-click **TestTrust** in the Explorer window. Create a file in the folder, and then delete the file you created. Close all open windows on Server2XX.

18. Remember, the trust you created was a one-way trust. It is not possible to give users in the W2k8AD1XX.local domain access to resources in the W2k8AD2XX.local domain. To verify this, on Server2XX open Active Directory Users and Computers.

19. Expand **W2k8AD2XX.local**, if necessary. Click **Builtin**, and double-click **Administrators** to open its Properties dialog box.

20. On Administrators Properties, click **Members**. Click **Add**. In the Select Users, Contacts, Computers, or Groups dialog box, click **Locations**. Notice that the W2k8AD1XX.local domain is not listed as an option from which you can choose accounts. Click **OK**, click **Cancel**, and then click **Cancel**. Close all open windows on both servers. Shut down Server2XX but stay logged on to Server1XX if you are going on to the next lab.

Review Questions

1. True or False? A one-way trust allows users in the trusting domain to be given permissions in the trusted domain.

2. Which of the following is true about external trusts?

   a. They are always two-way and transitive.

   b. They cannot be created between domains when one of the domains is the forest root.

   c. Once created, users have read-only permissions to all shares in the trusting domain.

   d. They can be one-way or two-way and they are not transitive.

3. Which of the following is true about accessing another domain's resources?

   a. You will always be able to see a list of shared resources in a domain even if there is no trust relationship with the domain.

   b. Once a trust is created, users in the trusting domain have access to resources in the trusted domain if they are given the appropriate permissions.

   c. Accounts in the trusted domain can be added to groups and DACLs in the trusting domain.

   d. If a two-way trust is created, the global Domain Users group in each domain is added to the domain local Users group in each domain.

4. True or False? The only way to create a trust between a Windows Server 2008 domain and a Windows NT domain is to use an external trust.

5. If you want users in DomainA to access resources in DomainB, but not vice versa, you should create a _____ trust.

Lab 10.4 Working with Operations Masters

Objectives

- Promote a server core server to domain controller
- Transfer the schema master to a server core server

Materials Required

This lab requires the following:

- Server1XX
- ServerCoreXX

Estimated completion time: **20 minutes**

Activity Background

FSMO role holders perform critical functions in a Windows domain; as such, administrators should be familiar with two important FSMO management operations: transferring and seizing. These two functions enable administrators to change the DC performing the FSMO role to make the Active Directory design more efficient and to recover from server failure.

Transferring an operations master role means moving the role's function from one server to another while the original server is still in operation. This transfer is generally done for one of the following reasons:

- The DC performing the role was the first DC in the forest or domain and, therefore, holds all domain-wide or domain- and forest-wide roles. Unless you have only one DC, distributing these roles to other servers is suggested.

- The DC performing the role is being moved to a location that isn't well suited for the role.

- The current DC's performance is inadequate because of the resources the FSMO role requires.

- The current DC is being taken out of service temporarily or permanently.

In this lab, you promote ServerCoreXX to a domain controller in the W2k8AD1XX domain and then use the command line program ntdsutil to transfer the Schema Master role to ServerCoreXX. Then you see how taking the schema master offline affects access to the schema.

Activity

1. Log on to Server1XX as Administrator, if necessary. Start ServerCoreXX and log on to the domain as Administrator.

2. ServerCoreXX is currently a domain member. You want to make ServerCoreXX a domain controller in the W2k8AD1XX.local domain. At the command prompt, type **dcpromo /?:promotion** and press **Enter**.

You see a list of options you can specify for installing AD DS. Scroll to read the complete list. Press the **spacebar** to quit.

3. Type **dcpromo /unattend /replicaOrNewDomain:replica /replicaDomainDNSName: W2k8AD1XX.local /ConfirmGC:Yes /RebootOnCompletion:Yes /SafeModeAdminPassword: Password01** and press **Enter**. (In the previous sentence, when you type the arguments, colons, and parameters, be sure *not* to include a space after the colons.) Supplying a username and password isn't necessary because you're already logged on to the domain as Administrator. DNS will not be installed as part of this Active Directory installation.

4. You see a number of information messages as AD DS is installed. When the installation is finished, ServerCoreXX should restart. Log on as **Administrator**.

5. At the command prompt, type **ntdsutil** and press **Enter**.

6. Type **roles** and press **Enter** to get the fsmo maintenance prompt.

7. Type **connections** and press **Enter** to get the server connections prompt.

8. Type **connect to server ServerCoreXX** and press **Enter**. Type **quit** and press **Enter**.

9. At the fsmo maintenance prompt, type **transfer schema master** and press **Enter**. Click **Yes**.

10. Type **quit** and press **Enter** twice to quit ntdsutil. Shut down ServerCoreXX by typing **shutdown /s /t 0** and pressing **Enter**.

11. On Server1XX, double-click the **Schema Management** MMC on the desktop that you created in Lab 4.3. It may take a while for it to start since the schema snap-in is trying to contact the schema master.

12. Expand **Active Directory Schema**, if necessary. Click **Classes**. Double-click **account** in the middle pane. Notice that all properties are grayed out. Click **Cancel**. Remember that you can make changes only on the schema master and that the Schema Management MMC is connected to Server1XX, which is no longer the schema master. Click **Attributes** and double-click **accountExpires**. Again, all properties are grayed out. Click **Cancel**.

13. Right-click **Active Directory Schema** and click **Operations Master**. Again, it may take a while before the dialog box is displayed. You will find that the Current schema master is shown as offline and the word ERROR is in place of the server name. See Figure 10-1. Click **Close**. Close Schema Management. When prompted to save console settings, click **No**.

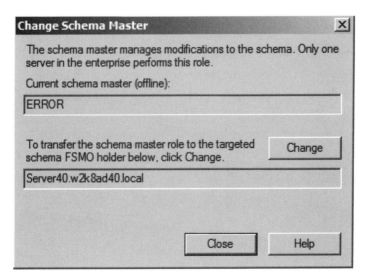

Figure 10-1 Schema Management showing the schema master offline

14. Restart ServerCoreXX. Once it has restarted, open Schema Management again. It should open much quicker this time and ServerCoreXX should be shown as the server to which the snap-in is connected.

15. Right-click **Active Directory Schema** and click **Operations Master**. You should see ServerCoreXX as the current schema master. Click **Close**.

16. Click **Classes** and double-click **account**. Notice that the Description and the two check boxes can now be changed. Click **Cancel**. Click **Attributes** and double-click **accountExpires**. Again, many of the properties can now be changed. Click **Cancel**.

17. To transfer the Schema Master back to Server1XX, you can repeat Steps 5–9, except in Step 8 change ServerCoreXX to Server1XX. Or, you can do it with the Schema Management snap-in. In this lab, you will transfer the Schema Master back to Server1XX using the Schema Management snap-in by following Steps 18 and 19.

18. Right-click **Active Directory Schema** and click **Change Active Directory Domain Controller**. In the Change Directory Server screen, click **Server1XX.W2k8AD1XX.local**. Click **OK**. Click **OK**.

19. Right-click **Active Directory Schema** and click **Operations Master**. Click **Change**. Click **Yes** when prompted. Click **OK** on the message stating Operations Master successfully transferred. Click **Close**.

20. Close Schema Management. Click **No** when prompted to save console settings. Shut down both servers.

Review Questions

1. True or False? Server Manager cannot be used to install the Active Directory DS role on Server Core.

2. Which of the following is true about the Schema Master?

   a. There is only one Schema Master per forest.

   b. There is only one Schema Master per domain.

   c. You can transfer the Schema Master only by using the command-line.

   d. You cannot transfer the Schema Master using the Schema snap-in.

3. Which of the following is true about Operations Master Roles?

   a. There is always only one RID master per forest.

   b. You must be logged on interactively to the domain controller that is the current operations master in order to transfer the role.

   c. There is only one domain naming master per forest.

   d. If you make changes to the schema while the schema master is offline, the changes will be written to the schema when the schema master comes back online.

4. True or False? The RID master must be available to continue creating Active Directory objects.

5. To manage Operations Master roles on a Server Core domain controller, you need to run the _____ command-line program.

CHAPTER ELEVEN

ACTIVE DIRECTORY CERTIFICATE SERVICES

Labs included in this chapter

- Lab 11.1 Deleting a Forest and Installing Active Directory Certificate Services
- Lab 11.2 Using the Certificates Snap-in to Request a Certificate
- Lab 11.3 Issuing and Testing an SSL Certificate for a Web Server

Microsoft MCTS Exam #70-640 Objectives

Objective	Lab
Configure the Active Directory Infrastructure	11.1
Install Active Directory Certificate Services	11.1
Manage Certificate Enrollments	11.2
Configure Active Directory Certificate Services	11.3

Lab 11.1 Deleting a Forest and Installing Active Directory Certificate Services

Objectives

- Delete an Active Directory forest
- Join a domain
- Install Active Directory Certificate Services

Materials Required

This lab requires the following:

- Server1XX
- Server2XX

Estimated completion time: **25 minutes**

Activity Background

Active Directory Certificate Services (AD CS) is a server role in Windows Server 2008 that is referred to as Certificate Services in previous Windows versions. AD CS provides the services for creating a public key infrastructure (PKI) that administrators can use to issue and manage public key certificates.

Best practices dictate that the AD CS role shouldn't be installed on a domain controller. In fact, for optimum security, AD CS should probably be the only role installed on the server. An enterprise certificate authority (CA) must be installed on a member server running Windows Server 2008 Enterprise or Datacenter Edition.

AD CS is installed in Server Manager by adding the AD CS role. During installation, you have several options, and your selections depend on how the CA will be used in your network. What's the name of your CA? Is it the root CA or a subordinate CA? Is it an enterprise or standalone CA? Will the CA issue certificates to users and devices or to other CAs? Keep in mind that many of the selections you make, including the CA name, can't be changed after AD CS is installed.

Activity

1. Start Server1XX. Start and log on to Server2XX as Administrator using **Password02**.

2. On Server2XX, click **Start** and type **dcpromo** in the Start Search box and press **Enter**.

3. On the Active Directory Domain Services Installation Wizard, click **Next**. Click **OK** when warned that this DC is a global catalog server.

4. Click **Delete the domain because this server is the last domain controller in the domain**. Click **Next**.

5. On the Application Directory Partitions screen, click **Next**. Click **Delete all application directory partitions on this Active Directory domain controller**, and then click **Next**.

6. On the Remove DNS Delegation screen, verify the check box is checked and click **Next**. Type **W2k8AD1XX\Administrator** in the User name field and **Password01** in the Password field and click **OK**.

7. In the Administrator Password screen, type **Password02** twice. Click **Next**. Click **Next** on the Summary screen. When prompted to restart, click **Restart Now**.

8. When Server2XX restarts, log on as **Administrator** and start Server Manager. Click **Roles**. Click **Remove Roles**.

9. In the Remove Roles Wizard, click **Next**. Uncheck the **Active Directory Domain Services** and **DNS Server** check boxes and click **Next**. Click **Remove**. Once removal is complete, you must restart the server. Click **Close**. Click **Yes** when prompted to restart now.

10. When Server2XX restarts, log on as **Administrator**. Once the Configuration Wizard finishes removing AD DS, click **Close**. You must change the IP configuration to use Server1XX as the DNS server. Open

a command prompt and type **netsh interface ipv4 add dnsserver "Local Area Connection" address=192.168.100.1XX index=1**

11. Click **Start**, right-click **Computer** and click **Properties**.

12. In System control panel, click **Change settings**. On the System Properties dialog box, click **Change**. Click the **Domain** option button. Type **W2k8AD1XX.local** and click **OK**.

13. On the Computer Name/Domain Changes prompt, type **Administrator** and **Password01** and click **OK**. Click **OK** on the welcome message. Click **OK** on the message stating that you must restart the computer. Click **Close**. Click **Restart Now**.

14. Once Server2XX restarts, log on to the domain as **Administrator**. To do so, click **Switch User** and click **Other User**. Type **W2k8AD1XX\administrator** in the User name box and type **Password01** in the Password box and click the arrow.

15. On Server2XX, start **Server Manager**. In the left pane, click **Roles**. In the right pane click **Add Roles**. Click **Next** in the welcome window.

16. In the Select Server Roles window, click **Active Directory Certificate Services**, and then click **Next**.

17. In the Introduction to Active Directory Certificate Services window, read the description and the paragraph under Things to Note. In particular, note that you can't change the computer name, join a different domain, or promote the server to a domain controller after the role is installed. Click **Next**.

18. In the Select Role Services window, the Certification Authority option is selected by default. Click to select **Online Responder**. The Online Responder role service requires the Web Server role service, so when you're prompted to add this role service, click **Add Required Role Services**. If the server were going to be a standalone root CA in a multilevel hierarchy, you would install only Certification Authority. You can't install NDES until the Certification Authority role has been installed. Click **Next**.

19. In the Specify Setup Type window, make sure **Enterprise** is selected. If you did not change this server's DNS address to the address of Server1XX, Enterprise is grayed out. Click **Next**.

20. In the Specify CA Type window, select **Root CA**, if necessary, and then click **Next**.

21. In the Set Up Private Key window, select **Create a new private key**, if necessary. If this CA were replacing a failed CA, you would have clicked "Select a certificate and use its associated private key." If you had a private key from a previous installation or from an external source, you would have clicked "Select an existing private key on this computer." Click **Next**.

22. In the Configure Cryptography for CA window, accept the default selections and click **Next**.

23. The next window requests a name for the CA. By default, the name is generated automatically to include the domain name and server name followed by "CA." For example, if the domain is W2k8AD99.local and the server name is Server199, the default CA name is W2k8AD99-Server199-CA. You can also enter the distinguished name suffix, but usually, the default is fine. Click **Next**.

24. In the Set Validity Period window, you can set the validity period of the certificate issued to this CA. The validity period should be specified in the certificate practice statement. The period you choose depends on how this CA is used and the types of certificates it will issue. If the certificate expires, the CA and any certificates it has issued are no longer valid. Certificates can be renewed as needed. Accept the default of 5 years, and then click **Next**.

25. In the Configure Certificate Database window, you can choose where certificates and the certificate log should be stored. If the CA will be used heavily, these two databases should be stored on separate drives and shouldn't be placed on the same drive as the Windows folder. For testing purposes, you can use the default location of C:\Windows\system32\CertLog for both databases. Click **Next**.

26. Because you chose to install the Online Responder role service, which requires the Web Server role service, the Web Server (IIS) window is displayed. Click **Next**.

27. You're prompted to select role services for the Web Server role service. If necessary, you can make changes to the default selections. For now, accept the defaults and click **Next**.

28. In the Confirm Installation Selections window, review the options you have chosen. You're also warned that you can't change the computer name or domain name after the CA has been installed. Click **Install**.

29. When the installation is finished, click **Close**.

11

30. In Server Manager, you probably have a warning event for AD CS. Click the **Active Directory Certificate Services** link next to the yellow warning message, and then double-click the **Warning** message. Read the event information. It explains how you can verify that the CA certificate was published correctly in Active Directory. Click **Close**.

31. Open a command prompt window, type **gpupdate /force**, and press **Enter** to update the certificate store (database where certificates are stored). After gpupdate has finished, type **certutil -viewstore** and press **Enter**. The View Certificate Store dialog box opens, listing all certificates currently published in Active Directory. Click the **W2k8AD1XX-Server2XX-CA** certificate, and then click the **View Certificate** button. Notice that the Issuer Statement button is grayed out. If you publish a CPS, this button becomes active and links to your CPS.

32. Click the **Details** tab to view more information about the certificate. Click the **Certification Path** tab, which shows the path through the CA hierarchy to the root CA where the certificate originates. In this case, only the current server is listed because you don't have a multilevel CA hierarchy. Click **OK**.

33. Click **OK** in the View Certificate Store dialog box to close it. Close all open windows.

34. Stay logged on to both servers if you are going on to the next lab, otherwise shut down both servers.

Review Questions

1. True or False? For the best security, you should install AD CS on a domain controller.

2. Which of the following describe an option when installing Active Directory Certificate Services? (Choose all that apply.)

   a. Selecting additional role services

   b. Should this be a root, distribution, or issuing CA

   c. Whether the server should be an Enterprise or Standalone CA

   d. Whether a new private key should be created

3. Which of the following is true when you uninstall DNS and demote the last DC in a domain?

   a. The DNS server address in your IP configuration automatically changes to the address of another DNS server.

   b. You only need to run the Remove Roles Wizard, not dcpromo.

   c. The server becomes a member of a domain with which it has a trust relationship.

   d. The domain is deleted.

4. True or False? The Online Responder role service requires the Web Server role service.

5. An Enterprise CA requires the _____ or _____ edition of Windows Server 2008.

Lab 11.2 Using the Certificates Snap-in to Request a Certificate

Objectives

- Manage certificate enrollments

Materials Required

This lab requires the following:

- Server1XX
- Server2XX
- ClientXX

Estimated completion time: **30 minutes**

Activity Background

By using the Certificates snap-in, users can request certificates that aren't configured for auto-enrollment. To do so, they must be logged on to the domain. The Request New Certificate wizard, that you run from the Certificates snap-in, lists the certificates available with this method.

The ability of users to request certificates using the Certificates snap-in can be used only with enterprise CAs. In this lab, you request a User certificate which can be used for EFS file encryption, secure e-mail, and client authentication.

Activity

1. Start Server1XX, if necessary. Click **Start**, point to **Administrative Tools**, and click **Certification Authority**.

2. Expand **W2k8AD1XX-Server2XX-CA**. Click **Certificate Templates**. The right pane lists the types of certificates that this CA may issue. Additional certificate types may be added if desired. In this list, the only certificates that a non-administrator user can be issued are the Basic EFS and the User certificate. You can view the full list of certificate templates by opening the Certificate Templates snap-in. Close the Certification Authority MMC.

3. Click **Start** and type **mmc** and press **Enter** in the Start Search box.

4. In the MMC console, click **File** and click **Add/Remove Snap-in**. In the Add or Remove Snap-ins window, click **Certificate Templates** and click **Add**. Click **OK**.

5. Click **Certificate Templates** in the left pane and then right-click the **User** certificate template in the middle pane and click **Properties**. Notice that the properties on the General tab are grayed out. You must create a copy of an existing template in order to change most of its properties. Notice that the Publish certificate in Active Directory option is selected.

6. Click the **Security** tab. In the Group or user names box, click **Domain Users**. Notice that the Enroll permission is allowed for Domain Users. See Figure 11-1. Click **Cancel**.

7. Right-click the **EFS Recovery Agent** template and click **Properties**. Click the **Security** tab. In the Group or user names box, click each of the groups listed. Notice that only Domain Admins and Enterprise Admins have the Enroll permission. In order for a certificate template to be available for a user to request it, the user must have the enroll permission. Click **Cancel**. Close the Certificate Templates MMC and click **No** when prompted to save the console.

8. Start ClientXX and log on to the domain from ClientXX as **DevUser1** using **Password03**.

9. On ClientXX, click **Start** and type **mmc** and press **Enter** in the Start Search box.

10. In the MMC console, click **File** and click **Add/Remove Snap-in**. In the Add or Remove Snap-ins window, click **Certificates** and click **Add**. Click **OK**.

11. To request a certificate, expand the **Certificates** node in the left pane. Right-click the **Personal** folder, point to **All Tasks**, and click **Request New Certificate**. The Certificate Enrollment wizard begins. Click **Next**.

12. The Request Certificates screen lists the certificate types you may request, as shown in Figure 11-2. Click **Details** in the User row. You will see a short description of the usage, application policies, and validity period.

13. Click **Properties**. You will see a window with five tabs. Explore each tab to see what options are available for the User certificate. Click the **Certification Authority** tab. Notice that this is the server you installed earlier. If more than one CA was available, you could choose which CA you want to use. Click **Cancel**.

14. On the Request Certificates window, click **User**. Click **Enroll**.

15. On the Certificate Installation Results window, click **Finish**.

16. You will now see a Certificates folder under the Personal folder in the Certificates snap-in. In the left pane, click to expand **Personal** and click **Certificates**. In the middle pane you will see the new certificate issued by W2k8AD1XX.Server2XX-CA. Under the Intended Purposes column you will see Encrypting File System, Secure Email, Client Authentication. Close the MMC. When prompted if you want to save console settings, click **No**.

17. Log on to the domain as **Administrator** from Server2XX. Click **Start**, point to **Administrative Tools**, and click **Certification Authority**.

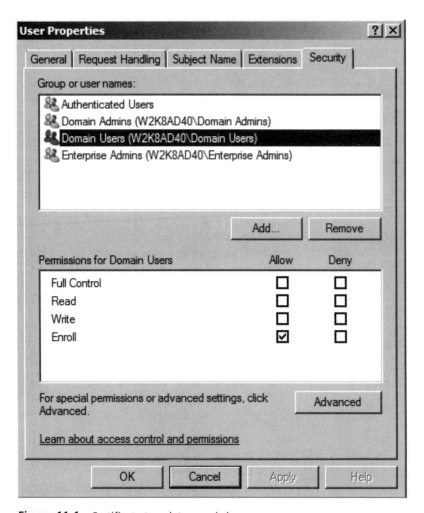

Figure 11-1   Certificate template permissions

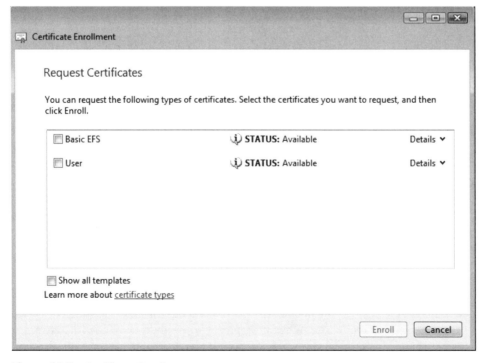

Figure 11-2   Certificate Enrollment

18. In the left pane, expand **W2k8AD1XX-Server2XX-CA**. Click the **Issued Certificates** folder. You will see the User certificate that was issued to DevUser1.

19. You worked with EFS certificates in Lab 6.1. When you encrypted a file, a self-signed EFS certificate was issued by the local system. In this case, the CA issued the certificate. Double-click the **certificate** issued to DevUser1 to view its properties.

20. Click the **Details** tab. Scroll down until you see the **Thumbprint** field. Note the first four numbers of the Thumbprint as you will be comparing this number shortly. Click **OK**. Close the Certificates mmc. If prompted to save the console settings, click **No**.

21. On ClientXX, click **Start** and click **Documents**. Create a text document and encrypt the document. When prompted whether to encrypt the file and its parent folder or the file only, click **Encrypt the file only** and click **OK**.

22. Right-click the document you just created and click **Properties** and click **Advanced**. Click **Details**. You should see that the Certificate Thumbprint is the same as the thumbprint you noted in Step 20. When more than one certificate exists for a user, the thumbprint is one way to distinguish them. Click **OK**. Close all open windows on ClientXX.

23. On Server1XX, open Active Directory Users and Computers. Browse to the **Development** OU and double-click **Dev User1**.

24. Click the **Published Certificates** tab on Dev User1's Properties page. The certificate for Dev User1 should be listed as shown in Figure 11-3. Click **OK**.

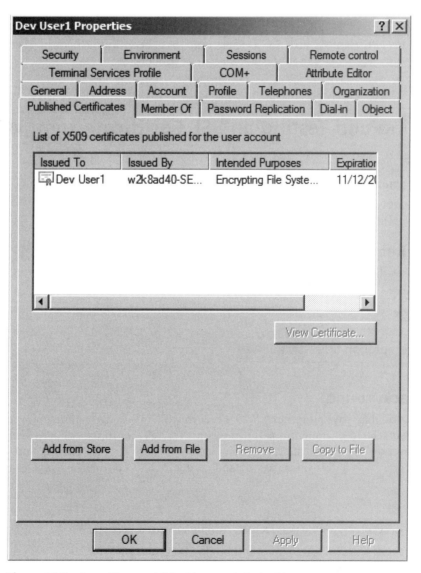

Figure 11-3   A certificate published in a user's Active Directory account

25. Close all open windows. Shut down ClientXX. Stay logged on to Server1XX and Server2XX if you are going on to the next lab, otherwise shut down both servers.

Review Questions

1. Which of the following is true about certificate requests?

    a. Users use the Certification Authority MMC to request a certificate.

    b. By default, users can enroll in all certificates listed in the Templates folder in Certification Authority.

    c. Users must have the enroll permission to request a certificate.

    d. Authenticated Users can request an EFS Recovery Agent certificate.

2. Which of the following is true about certificate templates?

    a. All templates listed in the Certificate Templates snap-in may be issued by the CA.

    b. A certificate template must be added to the Certificate Templates folder in the Certification Authority MMC before it can be issued.

    c. By default, there are four certificate templates available for enrollment by regular users.

    d. You cannot change the permissions set on a certificate template until it has been enabled.

3. True or False? The Thumbprint field of a certificate can help you identify a certificate when multiple certificates have been issued.

4. True or False? By default, a User certificate is published in Active Directory.

5. To view a certificate issued to a user that has been published in Active Directory, click the _____ tab in the user's account properties.

Lab 11.3 Issuing and Testing an SSL Certificate for a Web Server

Objectives

- Request a domain certificate for a Web site
- Test SSL access to a secured Web site

Materials Required

This lab requires the following:

- Server1XX
- Server2XX

Estimated completion time: **20 minutes**

Activity Background

In your forest, you may have an intranet Web server to which you want your employees to connect for corporate information and related documents. You may want the Web site to use secure communications, meaning that the Web site uses an SSL certificate to verify its identity and to encrypt information. In this lab, you configure the IIS Web server with a domain certificate and configure SSL options.

Activity

1. Log on to Server1XX and Server2XX as Administrator, if necessary.

2. On Server1XX, start Internet Explorer. The IIS Web service is running on Server2XX, so open a Web page on Server2XX by typing **http://Server2XX** in the address box of Internet Explorer and then pressing **Enter**. You should see the default Web page, which shows a logo for IIS7. Close Internet Explorer.

3. On Server2XX, click **Start**, point to **Administrative Tools**, and click **Internet Information Services (IIS)** Manager. Expand the **Server2XX** node.

4. In the middle pane, double-click **Server Certificates**. In the right pane, click **Create Domain Certificate**.

5. In the Distinguished Name Properties window, fill in the information in the following list. Your screen will look similar to Figure 11-4.

   - Common name: **Server2XX.W2k8AD1XX.local**
   - Organization: **Server 2008 AD Class**
   - Organizational unit: **Development**
   - City/locality: *Your city*
   - State/province: *Your state or province*
   - Country/region: *Your country*

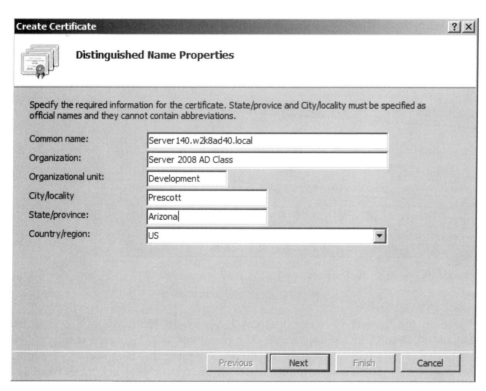

Figure 11-4   Create a Web Certificate Request

6. Once you have completed filling in the information, click **Next**.

7. On the Online Certification Authority screen, click **Select**. Click **W2k8AD1XX-Server2XX-CA** and click **OK**. In the Friendly name text box, type **W2k8 Class Certificate**, and then click **Finish**.

8. In the left pane of IIS Manager, click to expand the **Sites** node. Right-click **Default Web Site** and click **Edit Bindings**.

9. In the Site Bindings dialog box, click **Add**.

10. In the Add Site Binding dialog box, click the **Type** list arrow and click **https**. Click the **SSL certificate** list arrow, click **W2k8 Class Certificate**, and then click **OK**. Click **Close**.

11. In the left pane of IIS Manager, expand **Sites**, if necessary, and click **Default Web Site**. To test access to the Default Web Site using SSL, click **Browse *:443 (https)** in the right pane. A Web page explaining that there is a problem with the Web site's certificate is displayed. The page is displayed because the address you are using to access the Web site is localhost and the certificate specifies the site's full name.

12. Click **Continue to this website (not recommended)**. A warning message indicates that you are going to view pages over a secure connection. Click **OK**. You should see the same IIS7 logo you saw in Step 2.

13. Close Internet Explorer. In the middle pane of IIS Manager, double-click **SSL Settings**. In the SSL Settings dialog box, click **Require SSL**. Notice the options under Client certificates. You can have the Web server ignore, accept, or require client certificates. If you want client computers to connect to the Web server to verify their identity, you would select Require. For now, leave the default Ignore selected.

14. Click **Apply** in the Actions pane, and then click **Default Web Site** in the left pane. To test access to the Default Web Site without using SSL, click **Browse *:80 (http)** in the right pane. You should get a Web page that looks like Figure 11-5.

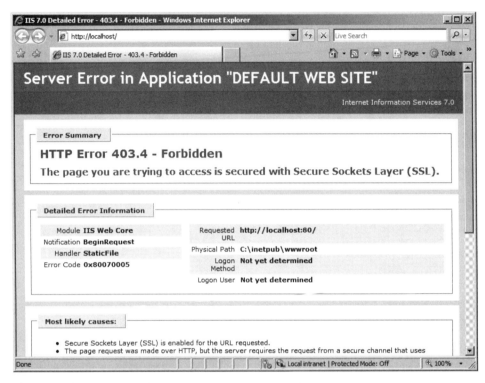

Figure 11-5   Access forbidden trying to access a site requiring SSL

15. Close Internet Explorer. On Server1XX, start Internet Explorer. In the address bar, type **https://Server2XX.W2k8AD1XX.local** and press **Enter**. The page with the IIS logo is displayed. Notice the padlock icon next to the address bar indicating that you are accessing this page securely using SSL. Click the **padlock** icon. You see a summary of the information for the certificate. Click **View certificates**. You see the certificate for the Web server. Click **OK**. Close **Internet Explorer**.

16. Using the method described in this lab to secure your Web site using SSL certificates works well when users accessing the site are in your network. Domain users' Web browsers will trust the certificate authority since it is a domain member. However, to secure a public Web server, you should create a certificate request in Step 4 and send the request to a well-known public certificate authority that is recognized by most Web browsers. Close all open windows on both servers. Shut down all your machines.

Review Questions

1. True or False? If a Web site is configured with an SSL certificate, all requests to the site must use the SSL protocol.

2. What port does the SSL protocol use by default?

   a. 80

   b. 443

   c. 334

   d. 21

3. Which of the following is true about using SSL to secure your Web site?

   a. You need to request a certificate from a public CA when domain users will be accessing your site.

   b. When you configure your site to require SSL, it will no longer accept page requests on port 80.

   c. If the Web site name on the certificate does not match the name in the address bar of your browser, you cannot view the Web page.

   d. The client must present a certificate to a Web server that uses SSL.

4. True or False? You can configure SSL settings to require a client to verify its identity.

5. When requesting a certificate for a Web server that will use a local online certificate authority, you should choose the _____ option in the Server Certificates section of IIS Manager.

11

CHAPTER TWELVE

ADDITIONAL ACTIVE DIRECTORY SERVER ROLES

Labs included in this chapter

- Lab 12.1 Install and Configure the AD LDS Server Role
- Lab 12.2 Install the AD RMS Role
- Lab 12.3 Install and Configure an RODC on Server Core

Microsoft MCTS Exam #70-640 Objectives

Objective	Lab
Configure Active Directory Lightweight Directory Service (AD LDS)	12.1
Configure Active Directory Rights Management Service (AD RMS)	12.2
Configure a forest or domain	12.3
Configure a read-only domain controller (RODC)	12.3

Lab 12.1 Install and Configure the AD LDS Server Role

Objectives

- Install AD LDS
- Create an AD LDS instance
- Use dsdbutil.exe, Ldp.exe, and ADSI Edit

Materials Required

- Server1XX
- Server2XX

Estimated completion time: **25 minutes**

Activity Background

AD LDS is installed on a Windows Server 2008 server by adding the Active Directory Lightweight Directory Services server role. It can be installed on all editions of Windows Server 2008 except Windows Web Server 2008 and Itanium. AD LDS can be installed on a domain controller, but it is not recommended.

AD LDS is first installed as a server role, and then one or more instances of AD LDS are created. Before AD LDS can be removed as a server role, all instances must be removed in Control Panel.

Each AD LDS instance has its own data store and communication ports and a unique service name; thus, to an application using AD LDS, each instance appears as a unique copy of the service. In this lab, you install AD LDS on Server2XX and create a unique instance that creates an application directory partition. Then you will experiment with the Ldp.exe, dsdbutil.exe, and ADSI Edit programs used to monitor and manage AD LDS.

Activity

1. Start Server1XX. Start Server2XX and log on to the domain as Administrator.

2. Open Server Manager and click the **Roles** node. In the right pane, click **Add Roles**. When the Add Roles Wizard starts, click **Next**.

3. In the Select Server Roles screen, check the **Active Directory Lightweight Directory Services** check box, and then click **Next**.

4. Read the information in the Introduction to Active Directory Lightweight Directory Services window, and then click **Next**.

5. In the Confirm Installation Selections window, click **Install**. In the Installation Results window, read the messages, and then click **Close**.

6. In Server Manager, under Roles Summary, click **Active Directory Lightweight Directory Services**.

7. In the Summary section, you see the message "No AD LDS instances have been created." Click the **Click here to create an AD LDS instance** link.

8. When the Active Directory Lightweight Directory Services Setup Wizard starts, click **Next**.

9. In the Setup Options window, make sure the default **A unique instance** is selected, and then click **Next**.

10. In the Instance Name window, type **ADLDS1** in the Instance name text box. Note that ADAM_ is added in front of the name you type automatically. Click **Next**.

11. In the Ports window, accept the defaults of 389 and 636. Note that each instance of AD LDS installed on the same computer requires different port numbers. Click **Next**.

12. In the Application Directory Partition window, click **Yes, create an application directory partition**. (If the directory-enabled application using this instance of AD LDS will create its own partition,

you should click **No**.) In the Partition name text box, type **cn=App1,dc=W2k8AD1XX,dc=local**, and then click **Next**.

13. Accept the default file locations, and then click **Next**.

14. You can use the default Windows service account or select a different account for running the AD LDS service. Accept the default **Network service account**, and then click **Next**.

15. In the AD LDS Administrators window, you can choose which user or groups have administrative permissions for AD LDS. Accept the default Currently logged on user, and then click **Next**.

16. You can import one or more LDIF files to configure aspects of the AD LDS application partition schema. If you're running an application that creates its own application directory, there's no need to import any of these files. You can also import LDIF files later. Click **Next**.

17. In the Ready to Install window, review your selections and click **Next** to install the AD LDS instance. When the installation is completed, click **Finish**.

18. You can list the AD LDS instances installed on a server using the dsdbutil command-line program. Open a command prompt. Type **dsdbutil** and press **Enter**.

19. From the dsdbutil prompt, type **list instances** and press **Enter**. You will see the ADLDS1 instance you created, the ports it is using, its status, and file locations. Type **?** and press **Enter** to get a list of commands supported by dsdbutil. Type **quit** and press **Enter**. Close the command prompt.

20. Another utility for managing AD LDS is Ldp.exe. Ldp.exe is a graphical utility for general AD LDS administration. To use Ldp.exe, in Server Manager, click the **AD LDS** role in the left pane, if necessary. In the right pane, under Advanced Tools, click the **Ldp.exe** link.

21. The Ldp window is blank—you must connect to the AD LDS service. On the menu bar, click **Connection** and click **Connect**. In the Connect window, type **Server2XX** and click **OK**. In the right pane, you should see information similar to Figure 12-1.

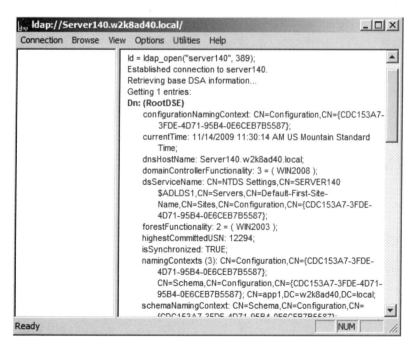

Figure 12-1   The ldp.exe utility

22. Click **Connection** and click **Bind**. Accept the defaults and click **OK**.

23. Click **View** and click **Tree**. You can type the distinguished name of the directory partition you wish to view or you can just click OK to view all partitions. Click **OK**.

24. In the left pane of Ldp, you see a listing of the partitions associated with the current instance of AD LDS. Double-click any of the partitions to view additional information about the partition.

25. Close Ldp by clicking **Connection** and **Exit**.

26. ADSI Edit is used to do low-level editing of Active Directory information in both AD DS and AD LDS. To use ADSI Edit, in Server Manager, click the **ADSI Edit** link in Advanced Tools.

27. Right-click the **ADSI Edit** node and click **Connect to**. The Connection Settings dialog opens. Type **App1** in the Name text box. Click **Select or type a Distinguished Name or Naming Context**. Type **cn=app1,dc=W2k8AD1XX,dc=local** in the text box below it. Under Computer, click **Select or type a domain or server** and type **Server2XX** and click **OK**.

28. In ADSI Edit, click to expand the **App1** node. Right-click the **Cn=app1,dc=W2k8AD1XX,dc=local** folder, point to **New**, and click **Object**. The six objects listed are the only object types you can create by default. However, additional object types can be created by extending the schema. See Activity 12-3 in the book that accompanies this manual for more information on extending the schema. Click **Cancel**.

29. Close all open windows. Stay logged on if you are going on to the next lab; otherwise, shut down both servers.

Review Questions

1. True or False? AD LDS can be installed on a domain controller.

2. Which of the following are reasons for deploying AD LDS? (Choose all that apply.)
   a. To support a directory-enabled application when schema modification on AD DS is not desired
   b. As a replacement for AD DS when you have a network of fewer than 50 users
   c. As a development environment for AD DS applications
   d. For integration with Active Directory Certificate Services

3. Which of the following is an AD LDS management tool? (Choose all that apply.)
   a. ADSI Edit
   b. dsdbutil.exe
   c. ldp.exe
   d. AD LDS Sites and Services

4. True or False? You can run only one instance of AD LDS on a single server.

5. To list the instances of AD LDS running on a server, run the _____ command-line tool.

Lab 12.2 Install the AD RMS Role

Objectives
- Install AD RMS
- Explore the AD RMS management console

Materials Required
- Server1XX
- Server2XX

Estimated completion time: **40 minutes**

Activity Background

In this lab manual, you have learned methods for allowing some end users to access information while disallowing other end users the same access. Access to digital information stored on computers can be allowed and disallowed by controlling who can authenticate to the servers storing information, assigning permissions to files and folders in the form of DACLs, and using encryption methods, such as EFS.

While access issues have been discussed in detail, what users can do with data after being granted access to it hasn't been given the same attention—until now. Active Directory Rights Management Service (AD RMS) helps administrators get a handle on this critical step in securing data. Whether protecting trade secrets, customer account information, or intellectual property, many organizations are struggling with this important facet of network security. With AD RMS, an administrator can create usage policies that define how a document can be used after a user accesses it. Actions such as copying, saving, forwarding, and even printing documents can be restricted. This lab steps you through the process of installing the AD RMS role and required role services.

Activity

1. Log on to Server1XX as Administrator, if necessary.

2. Create a new user with log on name **ADRMSsvc** in the Users folder. Assign the password of **RMSPass1** and make sure the account does not have to change the password at next log on.

3. Log on to the domain from Server2XX as Administrator, if necessary.

4. Start Server Manager and start the Add Roles Wizard. Click **Next**. On the Select Server Roles screen, click **Active Directory Rights Management Services**. Click **Add Required Role Services** when prompted and then click **Next**. Click **Next**.

5. On the Select Role Services screen, click **Next**. On the Create or Join an AD RMS Cluster screen, click **Next**.

6. On the Select Configuration Database screen, accept the default of using a Windows internal database and click **Next**.

7. On the Specify Service Account screen, click **Specify**. Type **ADRMSsvc** in the User name text box and type **RMSPass1** in the Password text box and click **OK**. Click **Next**.

8. On the Configure AD RMS Cluster Key Storage screen, click **Next**. On the Specify AD RMS Cluster Key Password screen, type **RMSPass1** twice and click **Next**. (Note: The password you use here need not be the password used for the service account.)

9. On the Select AD RMS Cluster Web Site screen, accept the Default Web Site and click **Next**.

10. On the Specify Cluster Address, accept the default of Use an SSL-encrypted connection because you already configured SSL for the Web site in Lab 11.3. In the Fully-Qualified Domain Name box type **W2k8AD1XX.local** and click **Validate**. Click **Next**.

11. Type **Server2XX-RMScert** in the Name text box for the certificate name and click **Next**.

12. On the Register AD RMS Service Connection Point screen, accept the default and click **Next**.

13. Click **Next** on the Web Server (IIS) screen. Review the additional IIS role services that will be installed and click **Next**.

14. On the Confirm Installation Selections screen, click **Install**. It will take quite a while to install all components. On the Installation Results screen, verify that all components were installed successfully and click **Close**.

15. Log off Server2XX and log back on. (The user that was logged on during AD RMS installation is automatically added to the AD RMS Enterprise Administrators group on Server2XX, so logging off and back on is necessary to update the account's credentials.)

16. To administer AD RMS, click **Start**, point to **Administrative Tools**, and click **Active Directory Rights Management Services**. You may get a Security Alert message. If so, click **View Certificate** and verify that the certificate is valid. Close the Certificate window and then click **Yes** to proceed.

17. View the recommended tasks in the Tasks box in the middle pane (see Figure 12-2). There are a number of additional steps needed to completely configure AD RMS that are beyond the scope of this lab. For more information, read the help available in the AD RMS MMC or go to http://technet.microsoft.com/en-us/library/cc771234%28WS.10%29.aspx. Close all open Windows.

18. This lab stepped you through the basics required to install and deploy AD RMS. The process is complex, but, at a minimum, you should know the starting point for implementing AD RMS and the reasons for doing so. For now, shut down Server2XX but leave Server1XX running if you are going on to the next lab.

12

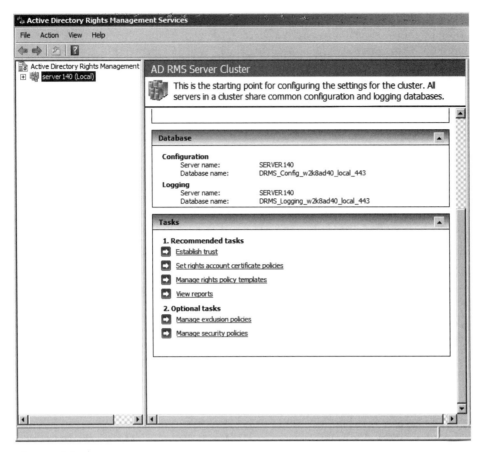

Figure 12-2 AD RMS management console

Review Questions

1. Which of the following is the primary purpose of AD RMS?

   a. To integrate with Active Directory-enabled applications

   b. To allow partner organizations access to your network resources

   c. To restrict how users can use the network data they access

   d. To specify which users or groups can access network data

2. Which of the following additional server roles must be installed on a server with AD RMS?

   a. DNS

   b. AD LDS

   c. AD DS

   d. Web Server (IIS)

3. True or False? AD RMS requires an SQL database to be installed on the AD RMS server.

4. True or False? The user account used to install AD RMS is added to the Enterprise Admins group.

5. When you specify the AD RMS cluster address, you should choose to use a(n) _____ connection so that communication with the AD RMS cluster is secure.

Lab 12.3 Install and Configure an RODC on Server Core

Objectives

- Demote a domain controller running Server Core
- Configure an RODC on a Server Core installation
- Create an answer file for a dcpromo unattended installation

Materials Required

- Server1XX
- ServerCoreXX

Estimated completion time: **25 minutes**

Activity Background

Because an RODC is meant to address the needs of a branch office, administrators can combine the RODC installation with another designed-for-branch-office installation: Server Core, which is Windows Server 2008 without a GUI. On a full Windows Server 2008 installation, you use Server Manager to install a role and Dcpromo.exe to start the Active Directory installation. On a Server Core installation, you start Dcpromo.exe from a command prompt with the /unattend installation option.

An RODC maintains a local user database, which allows users to log on to perform administrative tasks on the server without needing broader domain-wide permissions. A user logging on with a local user account has administrative capabilities only on the RODC. This feature is called administrator role separation and is configured with the Dsmgmt.exe command-line program.

In this lab, you first demote your ServerCoreXX server from a regular domain controller to a member server and then run an unattended dcpromo installation using an answer file. Then you configure administrator role separation by designating a domain user as a local administrator of the RODC.

Activity

1. Log on to the domain from ServerCoreXX as Administrator.

2. Before you can install an RODC, you must first demote ServerCoreXX to a member server. From the command prompt, type **dcpromo /AdministratorPassword:Password01** and press **Enter**.

3. Once dcpromo completes, the server will restart. Log on as Administrator using **Password01**. Next, you create an answer file for an unattended installation of an RODC.

4. At the command prompt, type **notepad** and press **Enter**. Type the following information into notepad, being sure to replace *XX* with your student number:

   ```
   [DCInstall]
   InstallDNS=Yes
   ConfirmGc=Yes
   RebootOnCompletion=No
   ReplicaDomainDNSName=W2k8AD1XX.local
   ReplicaOrNewDomain=ReadOnlyReplica
   SafeModeAdminPassword=Password01
   SiteName=SiteXX-Subnet100
   ```

5. Save the file as **c:\RODCAnswer.txt**.

6. In the command prompt type **dcpromo /unattend:c:\RODCAnswer.txt**, and press **Enter** to start the unattended installation.

7. Once the process completes, you can scroll through the output to see if there were any important status messages. You must restart the server to complete the process. Type **Shutdown /r /t 0** and press **Enter**.

8. ServerCoreXX is now an RODC for the W2k8AD1XX.local domain. Log on as Administrator.

9. Next, you want to configure administrator role separation. You can configure a domain user as an RODC administrator without giving the user broader administrative authority. From the command prompt on ServerCoreXX, type **dsmgmt** and press **Enter**.

10. At the dsmgmt prompt, type **local roles** and press **Enter**.

11. At the local roles prompt, type **list roles** and press **Enter**. The roles you can assign to a user, including Administrators, Backup Operators, and so forth, are displayed.

12. Type **add devuser1 administrators** and press Enter.

12

13. Type **show role administrators** and press **Enter**. The W2k8AD1XX\DevUser1 account should be listed.

14. Type **quit** and press **Enter**, and then type **quit** and press **Enter** again. DevUser1 is now a local administrator for the RODC, allowing the user to perform administrative tasks related only to the RODC such as performing backups, installing devices, configuring networking, and so forth.

15. Close all open windows on Server1XX. Shut down both Server1XX and ServerCoreXX unless you are going on immediately to the next chapter.

Review Questions

1. True or False? An RODC can be installed only on a Windows Server 2008 Server Core installation.

2. You want a user located at the branch office where you have installed an RODC to be able to perform server administrative tasks on the RODC without your giving him or her broader administrative rights in the domain or on other servers. What should you do?

   a. Put the server in an OU and delegate control of the OU to the user.

   b. Add the user to the Power Users group.

   c. Configure administrator role separation.

   d. Add the user to the Server Operators group.

3. Which of the following is true about an RODC installation?

   a. It can be the first domain controller in your domain.

   b. It requires Windows Server 2003 or later.

   c. It cannot be a global catalog server.

   d. There must be a writable DC running Windows Server 2008 in the domain first.

4. True or False? An Active Directory-integrated DNS zone on an RODC is also read-only.

5. To configure a local administrator to log on to an RODC to perform administrative tasks, run the _____ command.

CHAPTER THIRTEEN

SERVER MANAGEMENT AND MONITORING

Labs included in this chapter

- Lab 13.1 Using Event Viewer on Windows Server 2008

- Lab 13.2 Subscribe to Events and Create a Task When a New Event Is Created

- Lab 13.3 Monitoring Active Directory Replication

Microsoft MCTS Exam #70-640 Objectives

Objective	Lab
Monitor Active Directory	13.1, 13.2, 13.3

Lab 13.1 Using Event Viewer on Windows Server 2008

Objectives

- Use Event Viewer to view event logs

Materials Required

This lab requires the following:

- Server1XX

Estimated completion time: **15 minutes**

Activity Background

Administrators use Event Viewer to examine event log entries generated by system services and applications. A typical event log can contain hundreds or thousands of events, but usually, administrators are interested only in events that indicate a problem.

You can examine several log files in Event Viewer, including the Application, Security, and System logs. For Active Directory events, you can view the Directory Service log.

AD DS generates many events, but you're usually most interested in warning and error events. By clicking the Level column header, you can sort events and group them by level to spot the most serious events easily. When an event is selected, descriptive information about it is displayed in the bottom pane of the General tab. In this lab you explore Event Viewer, use filtering options, and custom views.

Activity

1. Start Server1XX and log on as Administrator if necessary.

2. Start Event Viewer by clicking **Start, Administrative Tools, Event Viewer.**

3. In the left pane, you have four folders from which to choose. Expand **Windows Logs**. You will see the following logs: Application, Security, Setup, System, and Forwarded Events.

4. Click the **Application** log. You will probably see a number of events displayed in the middle pane. Click the **Security** log. You will see a number of Logon and Logoff events created because logon/logoff events are audited by default. Most of what you see will be Audit Success events.

5. To view only Audit Failure events related to logon, click **Find** in the action pane. In the Find what text box, type **Audit Failure** and click **Find Next**. You should be able to find an Audit Failure message. Note the Event ID shown in the Event ID column. This ID should be 4625 for an Audit Failure logon event. Click **Cancel**.

6. In the Action Pane, click **Filter Current Log**. Click in the text box that currently says <All Event IDs> and type **4625**. Click **OK**. You will now only see events with Event ID 4625. You can also filter on keywords, users, computers, and other information. Click **Clear Filter** in the Actions pane to restore the normal view.

7. In the left pane, expand **Applications and Services Logs**. You will see a number of additional logs including DFS Replication, Directory Service, and DNS Server.

8. Click the **Directory Service** log. Click **Filter Current Log** and click the **Critical, Error,** and **Warning** boxes in the Event level section. Click **OK**. You will likely see some Warning and Error events. Double-click any of the events and read the information displayed.

9. Click **Event Log Online Help** in the Event Properties dialog box. You are informed that information will be sent across the Internet. Click **Yes**. An Internet Explorer window opens. Depending upon the event that you opened, you may or may not get additional information about the event from the Microsoft site. Close Internet Explorer. Click **Close** to close the event properties.

10. In the left pane, click **Custom Views**. In the middle pane are two preconfigured custom views: Administrative Events and Server Roles. Custom Views allows you to view events across multiple log files. You can create your own custom views as well. Double-click **Administrative Events**. You will see all Critical, Error, and Warning messages from all administrative logs.

11. In the middle pane, click the **Level** column header to sort events by level. To sort by the log file from which the event originates, click the **Source** column header.

12. In the left pane, click **Server Roles**. You will see three sub-views. Double-click Active **Directory Domain Services**. Any events that relate to AD DS from any of the logs will be displayed in the middle pane.

13. In the left pane, right-click **System** under Windows Logs and click Clear Log. You will have the option to Save and Clear, Clear, or Cancel. If you want to save the log for future reference, click Save and Clear. For now, just click **Clear**.

14. Right-click **Security** log and click **Properties**. On the General tab, you will see the path to the log file, the maximum size, and options of what should be done when the maximum size is reached. Be careful with the Security log. If you select the *Do not overwrite events* option and the log becomes full, only the Administrator will be able to log on to the server until the log has been manually cleared. Click **OK**.

15. Close all open windows. Stay logged on to Server1XX if you are going on to the next lab; otherwise, shut the server down.

Review Questions

1. True or False? Event logs can be sorted by the event ID.

2. Which of the following is true about Event Viewer? (Choose all that apply.)

    a. The Windows Logs include the Application, Security, and System logs.

    b. Auditing events are found in the System log.

    c. When the maximum size of a log file is reached, you must manually clear it.

    d. Logon/logoff events are audited by default.

3. Which of the following is true about events? (Choose all that apply.)

    a. Events from multiple logs can be combined into a single view.

    b. Event level categories are Low, Medium, and High.

    c. One of the predefined custom views is Network Events.

    d. You can choose to automatically archive a log when it becomes full.

4. True or False? If the Security log becomes full, you must boot into safe mode and clear the log.

5. To see logs generated by AD DS, click the _____ log.

Lab 13.2 Subscribe to Events and Create a Task When a New Event Is Created

Objectives

- Subscribe to events that occur on another computer
- Create a task when an event is forwarded from another computer

Materials Required

This lab requires the following:

- Server1XX
- ServerCoreXX

Estimated completion time: **40 minutes**

Activity Background

Event Viewer allows you to connect to another computer to view that computer's events logs. However, you may be interested in seeing certain types of events from other computers without having to connect to those computers. In such cases, you would use event subscriptions, which allow you to have events from one or more computers forwarded to the event log of another computer. You can specify from which logs and what types of events you wish to have forwarded. In addition, you can create a task associated with the receipt of an event. You can have the task send an e-mail, run a program, or display a message when an event occurs. In this lab, you will set up an event subscription with ServerCoreXX and then create a task that will display a message when an event is forwarded from ServerCoreXX to Server1XX.

Activity

1. Start ServerCoreXX. Log on to Server1XX as Administrator, if necessary.

2. On Server1XX, start Event Viewer. In the left pane, right-click **Subscriptions** and click **Create Subscription**. You will see a message about starting the Windows Event Collector Service. Click **Yes**.

3. In the Subscription Properties dialog, type **ServerCoreXX errors and warnings** in the Subscription name text box. Notice that the Destination log is set to Forwarded Events by default (see Figure 13-1).

4. Verify the Collector initiated option button is selected and click **Select Computers**.

5. Click **Add Domain Computers**. In the Select Computer dialog, type **ServerCoreXX** and click **Check Names**. Click **OK**. Click **Test** to verify connectivity with ServerCoreXX. Click **OK** on the Connectivity test succeeded message. Click **OK**.

6. On the Subscription Properties screen, click the **Select Events** button.

7. On the Query Filter screen, click the **Critical**, **Error**, and **Warning** event level boxes.

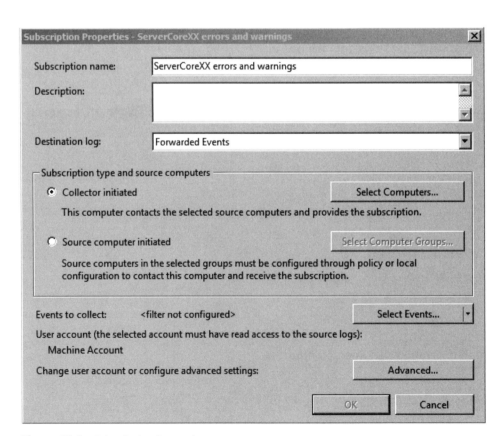

Figure 13-1 Subscription Properties

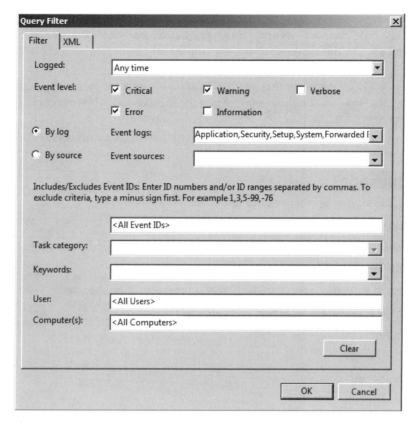

Figure 13-2 Query Filter

8. Click the **By log** option button, if necessary, and click the selection box arrow. Click the **Windows Logs** box to collect events from the primary log files. Notice that you can further filter the subscription by event ID, keywords, user, and computer (see Figure 13-2). Click **OK**.

9. Click the **Advanced** button. In the Advanced Subscription Settings screen, click the **Specific User** option button. Click the **User and Password** button and type **Password01** in the Password box. Click **OK**. Click **OK** to close the Advanced Subscription Settings screen. Click **OK** to close Subscription Properties.

10. In the left pane, click the **Subscriptions** node. In the middle pane of Event Viewer, you will see the name of the subscription. You can create additional subscriptions for additional servers or using different filter properties if desired. Make sure the subscription is highlighted in the middle pane, and in the right pane, click **Runtime Status**. Verify that the current status is Active. Click **Close**.

11. It may take a while before you see any events. However, to test your subscription, you can manually create an event. On ServerCoreXX, log on as Administrator if necessary. In the command prompt type **eventcreate /T Error /ID 1000 /L Application /D "Event to test Event Viewer subscriptions"** and press **Enter**. That command will create an Error level event in the Application log.

12. It can take a few minutes before the event is forwarded to the Forwarded Events log on Server1XX. While you are waiting, you can use Event Viewer to connect to ServerCoreXX. On Server1XX, in the left pane of Event Viewer, right-click the **Event Viewer** node and click **Connect to Another Computer**. Type **ServerCoreXX** in the text box and click **OK**.

13. Expand **Windows Logs** and click the **Application** log. You should see the Error event you just created. To connect back to Server1XX, repeat Step 12, except click the **Local computer** option button rather than typing the computer name.

14. Expand **Windows Logs** and click **Forwarded Events**. If the event is not listed, wait a few minutes, right-click **Forwarded Events** and click **Refresh**. Eventually, the event should be displayed.

15. You can also cause an alert to be sent when a subscribed event arrives. In Event Viewer, right-click the **Forwarded Events** log, and click **Attach a Task To this Log**.

16. The Create Basic Task Wizard starts. Accept the default name and click **Next**. Click **Next** again.

17. On the Action screen, click the **Display a message** option button. Click **Next**.

18. On the Display a Message screen, in the Title text box, type **A New Event Has Been Forwarded**. In the Message box, type **An event has arrived in the Forwarded Events log**. Click **Next**. Click **Finish**. On the message informing you that the task has been created, click **OK**. Note that you can edit this task by opening Task Scheduler and double-clicking the task.

19. On ServerCoreXX, create another event by following Step 11. When the message arrives in the Forwarded Events log, the message should display. When the message is displayed, click **OK** to close the message. Again, it may take several minutes before the event is forwarded.

20. Close all open windows on Server1XX. Keep both Server1XX and ServerCoreXX running if you are going on to the next lab.

Review Questions

1. Which of the following is true about Event Viewer subscriptions?

   a. Only error events can be subscribed to.

   b. By default, the subscribed events are placed in the Forwarded Events log.

   c. Information events cannot be subscribed to.

   d. Subscribed to events appear immediately on the subscribing server.

2. Which of the following is an action you can select to occur when an event is logged? (Choose all that apply.)

   a. Create a new event in the event log

   b. Start a program

   c. Send an e-mail

   d. Display a message

3. True or False? You can have only one active Event Viewer subscription.

4. True or False? You can choose more than one computer from which to have events forwarded.

5. To create a new event manually, use the _____ command.

Lab 13.3 Monitoring Active Directory Replication

Objectives

- Use repadmin to view replication status and force replication
- Use dcidag to diagnose DNS and Active Directory problems
- Use Performance Monitor to view real-time replication statistics

Materials Required

This lab requires the following:

- Server1XX
- ServerCoreXX

Estimated completion time: **20 minutes**

Activity Background

Correct and timely replication of Active Directory objects is critical to the operation of a Windows Server 2008 domain. Replication statistics can be monitored with Performance Monitor. Additional command-line tools include repadmin and dcdiag. In this lab you will use all three tools to monitor replication, force replication, and view the status of replication.

Activity

1. Start Server1XX, if necessary, and log on as Administrator. Start ServerCoreXX, if necessary, and log on as Administrator.

2. On ServerCoreXX, type **repadmin /?** and press **Enter**. Scroll through the help screen to get an idea of the options available for this command.

3. Type **repadmin /replsummary** and press **Enter** to get a summary display of replication status. This command will show you if there are any replication errors on each domain controller.

4. Type **repadmin /showrepl** and press **Enter**. You will see output similar to Figure 13-3.

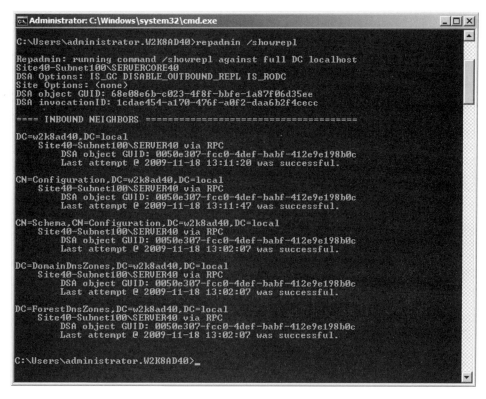

Figure 13-3   Output of repadmin /showrepl

5. Study the output of the repadmin command. You can see in the line that starts with DSA Options that outbound replication is disabled and that the DC is an RODC. Under the INBOUND NEIGHBORS line, you will see five sections of output. The first line of each section specifies the Active Directory partition that is being replicated. The second line specifies the replication partner.

6. To force replication between two DCs type **repadmin /replicate ServerCoreXX Server1XX dc=W2k8AD1XX,dc=local /readonly** and press **Enter**. The /readonly parameter is needed when one of the DCs is an RODC. This command can come in especially handy when testing replication between sites.

7. Another option for repadmin is /syncall, which can perform a synchronization amongst all the DCs and display the results. Type **repadmin /syncall /APe** and press **Enter**. The /A option specifies all partitions, the P option specifies a push replication, and the e option specifies the entire enterprise including across sites. The output provides details for each directory partition.

8. To perform general diagnostic tests for overall status and health of Active Directory, you can use the dcdiag command. To test overall DNS operation, type **dcdiag /test:DNS** and press **Enter**.

9. Type **dcdiag /test:Replications** and press **Enter** to test for error-free replication. To run all the primary tests, type **dcdiag** and press **Enter**.

10. You can also use Reliability and Performance Monitor to monitor Active Directory replication performance. On Server1XX, click **Start,** point to **Administrative Tools,** and click **Reliability and Performance Monitor**.

11. In the left pane, click **Performance Monitor**. Click the red X to delete the % Processor Time counter. Click the green **(+)plus** sign to add a new counter.

12. In the Add Counters screen, scroll up until you see Directory Services. Expand **Directory Services**. Click **DRA Inbound Bytes Not Compressed (Within Site)/sec** and click **Add**. Click **DRA Inbound Bytes Total/sec** and click **Add**. Click **DRA Outbound Bytes Total/sec** and click **Add**. Click **OK**. Those are some of the key counters for replication between DCs in the same site.

13. The only way to see some meaningful information is if you were to make a number of Active Directory changes. One way to do this is to delete several objects. Open Active Directory Users and Computers. Click **OU1**. In the right pane, click the **first object,** and while holding the **Shift** key, click the **last**

13

object so that all objects are selected. Press **Delete** on the keyboard or click the red **X** delete icon on the menu bar.

14. When prompted, if you are sure you want to delete the objects, click **Yes**. Return to the Reliability and Performance Monitor window. Within 15 seconds, you should see a peak for the DRA Outbound Bytes as in Figure 13-4.

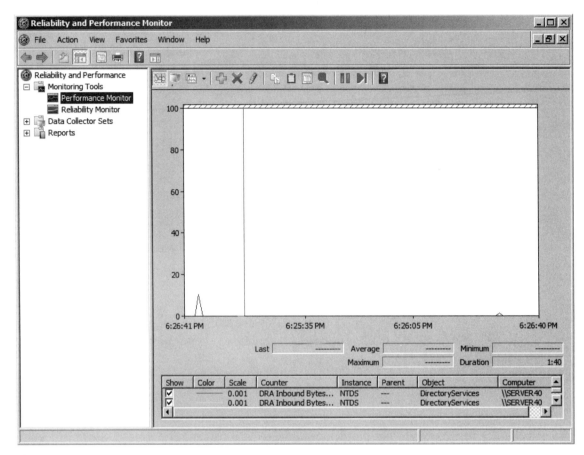

Figure 13-4 Monitoring Active Directory replication with Performance Monitor

15. Close all open windows. Shut down both servers.

Review Questions

1. True or False? An RODC will always have both inbound and outbound replication.

2. Which command will force replication between two specific domain controllers?

    a. repadmin /syncall

    b. repadmin /replicate

    c. replmon /replication

    d. replmon /syncall

3. Which of the following can be used to test replication?

    a. dcdiag /test:Replications

    b. repadmin /test /allrepl

    c. replmon /testrepl

    d. perfmon /testDRA

4. True or False? Performance Monitor can be used to see real-time performance data of Active Directory replication.

5. To test overall DNS operation, type _____ at a command prompt.